The
Country
Called
Life

The Country Called Life

More Reflections for Living

Lou Guntzelman

Saint Mary's Press
Christian Brothers Publications
Winona, Minnesota

Genuine recycled paper with 10% post-consumer waste.
Printed with soy-based ink.

The publishing team included Michael Wilt, development editor; Brooke E. Saron, copy editor; Barbara Bartelson, production editor and typesetter; Cären Yang, cover designer; produced by the graphics division of Saint Mary's Press.

Cover painting by Charles Perkalis

The acknowledgments continue on page 131.

Printed in the United States of America

Printing: 9 8 7 6 5 4 3 2 1

Year: 2008 07 06 05 04 03 02 01 00

ISBN 0-88489-380-4

Library of Congress Cataloging-in-Publication Data

Guntzelman, Lou.
     The country called life: more reflections for living / Lou Guntzelman.
     p. cm.
ISBN 0-88489-380-4
1. Christian life—Catholic authors. I. Title.
BX2350.2 .G85 2000
242—dc21
                                                        99-050787

Dedicated to my nieces and nephews.
How much less my life would be without them!
Jennifer
Laura
Mike
Tom

I wish to thank those who helped with the compilation of this book by the gifts of their time, talents, proofing skills, editing, and suggestions: Carol Fibbe, Mary Ellen Guntzelman, and Beverly Williamson. Appreciation is also offered to Sue McHugh, publisher of *The Community Press,* for the weekly opportunity to place my insights before so many people.

Contents

Introduction

THERE ARE TWO fundamental ways we can exist in the world, says German philosopher Martin Heidegger. He calls them the state of forgetfulness of being and the state of mindfulness of being.

When we live in the state of forgetfulness of being, we overlook and *forget* the richer, deeper part of what is really taking place. It's like competing in the Olympics and thinking of it as just a neighborhood game; it's like being married and remaining blasé to the passion, love, and relationship that could be shared. When we exist with forgetfulness of being, we miss the mystery and meaning of life. We even miss much of ourself. We skim along the surface of life rather than experience it in depth. We remain part of the veneer that coats existence, the everyday diversions, the world of things and distractions. We talk a lot, but we are really just chattering.

Heidegger describes that state of living as inauthentic, as an existence in which we are significantly unaware of ourself and of the ongoing authorship of our life. We seem to tranquilize ourself and set our life on automatic pilot. We go with the flow. We are more concerned with the *way* things are than *that* they are.

When we live in the state of mindfulness of being, we are aware of the wonder of being unique people who are not only alive, participating in the thrill of existence, but responsible for our own qualitative growth. We are more in touch with our depths and our ability for change and self-creation. The potential of an Olympic day occurs every day. We take hold of both our possibilities and our limits, our freedom and our nothingness, and the anxiety that goes with them. One chief

9

characteristic of this state is that we are not unduly upset with the *way* things are; rather, we marvel much more *that* they are.

For example, in the state of forgetfulness of being, we tend to make big things out of little things. We become unduly irritated at the bird that leaves droppings on our patio furniture—at the *way* things are. But the person who is mindful of being looks at the same bird droppings in a different way. The presence of the droppings may be unfortunate, but it is not unsettling. The mindful person is intrigued by the existence of the birds themselves—*that* they are.

These short essays are written to contribute to a state of mindfulness of being—to encourage us to look anew at common things and see more than the ordinary, to look at ourself and become acquainted with the profundity we see, to taste the experiences and variations of life and find in their midst meaning, wisdom, and more intense life.

The new millennium and the momentousness of our times invite us to be more than observers of existence, more than forgetful passersby. The flow of time urges us to be mindfully and passionately involved, to experience and understand, to move deeper into life as thoughtful participants. Rainer Maria Rilke expresses well God's invitation to enter into the existence given us:

> God speaks to each of us as he makes us,
> then walks with us silently out of the night.
> These are the words we dimly hear:
>
> You, sent out beyond your recall,
> go to the limits of your longing.
> Embody me.
>
> Flare up like flame
> and make big shadows I can move in.
>
> Let everything happen to you: beauty and terror.
> Just keep going. No feeling is final.
> Don't let yourself lose me.
>
> Nearby is the country they call life.
> You will know it by its seriousness.
>
> Give me your hand.

"It's All Straw!"

THOMAS AQUINAS WAS ONE of the greatest intellectual scholars in the history of the Catholic church. A thirteenth-century philosopher and theologian, he wrote voluminously, and his insights still influence theology today.

Curiously, though endowed with personal brilliance and a fluent pen, he never completed his most noteworthy work, the *Summa Theologiae*. Aquinas reached a point in his life when he stopped writing. Looking back over his accumulated works, he proclaimed, "It's all straw!" He realized how little he or we would ever know about God. Aquinas's wisdom had overtaken his knowledge.

The more intellectually naive we are, the more we think we know God. In my younger years, I thought I had a pretty good fix on God. How intellectually arrogant and simplistic I was. Not that I'm much better now, but at least I know that I don't know. I possess barely a hint of God's magnificence and transcendence. I realize that God is more *un*like my way of thinking about God than like it.

We have a constant tendency to make God similar to ourself but just a little bit better. Psychological analysis reminds us that we hardly know ourself. Yet we feel bold enough to take the little we know about ourself, extrapolate it, shine it up, and say, "God's like me, only bigger." Human life is an analogy for God. How foolish! Speaking of God as just a more sophisticated example of ourself is the kataphatic way of talking about God. We attribute to God all the good qualities we see in humans, intensified to the highest possible degree. We talk *about* God. When we speak kataphatically, we cannot express God's

11

innermost reality, God's very life. No created thing can ever adequately mirror the very reality of God.

Another way of trying to talk about God is the apophatic way, the way of negation. This way of speaking about God is the flip side of analogy. We know by not knowing. We realize that our words, images, and definitions are inadequate for describing God, and they may in fact be a hindrance. The apophatic way of speaking about God takes us into the mystery of God openhandedly and silently.

Think how glibly we traditionally speak of God. We commonly use male pronouns, yet God is as much "she" as "he." We think God is "up there," whereas God is closer to us than we are to ourself. Confined in the flow of time, we go to bed every night and think of tomorrow. With God there is always a tomorrow. God is not affected by the limitations of time. All of existence is present to God.

Every day we make countless choices. And though we truly are free to choose, God knows our choices before we make them. God sees us at every moment—when we are born, when we die, and at each moment along the way. "Even before a word is on my tongue, / O LORD, you know it completely" (Psalm 139:4).

Human logic says that if we are good people, we will be healthy, wealthy, and wise; God's logic often uses suffering, illness, and need to make us wise. We think of God as immensely large, but God shows up in the smallest of places. We say God is powerful, yet sometimes God seems weak by our standards. We suspect that God is not with us at the very times God is closest. When we're confused and lost, God may be leading us down a precise path. God is the paradox yet to be revealed.

What does all that mean to our life? It means that we are on an exciting adventure. An unimaginable Being is benignly disposed toward us, loving us, yearning for our awareness and our heart. We need to open ourself to let God make contact with us. We can trust God with our fragile, imperfect self. We can desire God's fascinating beauty. In *The Golden Key,* George MacDonald acknowledges the hint of this mysterious Being in our mind:

> And now Tangle felt that there was something
> in her knowledge which was not yet in her understanding . . .
> and the longer she looked the more an indescribable vague intelligence went on rousing itself in her mind.

God is the surprise that puts our best dreams to shame.

"It's April, and I am blind"

A YOUNG MAN SAT cross-legged on the grass of a busy university campus. Red and yellow tulips stood nearby, tree leaves had turned green again, and a glance in any direction caught visual mists of delicate purples, yellows, and white. The man sitting in the grass was a beggar, the quiet type, easily overlooked. Yet people noticed him. Most dropped something in his box. What drew the response he received? A simple sign someone had printed for him that read, "It's April, and I am blind."

It takes a jolt, sometimes, to make us notice the beauty that surrounds us. We look *past* things, not *into* things. Preoccupied with busyness, worries, and routine, we blind ourself to springtimes and snowfalls. We miss more than the blind beggar does. At least he compensates by delighting in the breeze that tousles his hair, listening to the birds, and noticing the variety of tones in the human voices that fill the air around him.

Reveling in beauty is a distinctly human ability. Every human needs it and its call to higher realms. Psychologist Rollo May says, "Beauty is serene and at the same time exhilarating; it increases one's sense of being alive." He continues, "When we are before an image of beauty, we instinctively remain silent."

Beauty leads us places we need to go to become more human. It coaxes us to pause and enter into these places. If we're unhurried and reflective enough to go in, we discover that beauty is a doorway. It opens into a deeper realm of life. Beauty is a bit of eternity born into human existence. Enjoying beauty melts time away. When absorbed in beauty, we conclude, "I could live or die tomorrow, but *now I have this moment.*"

As was apparent in his early life, Saint Augustine was a sensual person. His advice to the person looking for God is to begin by looking at the beauty of the surrounding world:

> And I said to all these things in my external environment: 'Tell me of my God who you are not, tell me something about him.' And with a great voice they cried out: 'He made us' (Ps. 99:3). My question was the attention I gave to them, and their response was their beauty.

We too are sensual creatures, equipped to appreciate the sights, sounds, and scents around us. If our wisdom grows, we learn to let the beautiful lead us into the pleasures of the spirit. Though our discovery of God ends in our inner self, for most of us it begins in the world outside.

It's April. Am I blind? Will this springtime pass by without my noticing her beauty? Will the flowers that bloom for me remain wall-flowers because I did not dance with them? Will the green of new life go unnoticed in the glow of my computer monitor? Will the marvelous human bodies walking by me on a warm evening fail to remind me of the marvel of my own body?

Mention God and most people immediately think of law or dogma. Not many connect God and beauty in the same breath. Saint Augustine did. After living the first half of his life in a hedonistic way, discon-necting beauty and pleasure from their Maker, he eventually became en-amored by the beauty of God. He writes passionately and sensually of God in his *Confessions:*

> Late have I loved you, O Beauty so ancient and so new, late have I loved you. You were within me and I was outside, where I rushed about wildly searching for you like some monster loose in your beautiful world. You were with me, but I was not with you. Then you called me. You shouted to me, you wrapped me in your splen-dor. You broke past my deafness, you bathed me in your light, you sent my blindness reeling. You gave out such a delightful fragrance and I drew it in and came breathing hard after you. I tasted, and it made me hunger and thirst. You touched me, and I burned to know your peace.

This is quite a powerful statement about a God we consider so dull, so unexciting, so separate from beauty and the sensual. Maybe God is April, and we're blind!

Peace: One Benefit of Believing

HE IS SEVENTY-THREE years old, very alert and active. He has a number of physical infirmities that cause some discomfort, the worst of which is an arrhythmia of the heart. Still he is gentle, optimistic, sensitive to others, and has a wonderful sense of humor.

However, because of his heart condition, he lives with the almost-forgotten-but-never-gone realization that at any time his heart could jump into its strange pattern of beats. A doctor could probably get it stabilized again—or he could die.

That last thought could increase the fear and stress level of many people. They might become afraid to do anything or go anywhere. They might live a half-life. Yet this man sleeps well; enjoys life with his wife, children, and grandchildren; works in the yard; and vacations around the country. How does he do it?

I found out the last time I visited him. As I was leaving, I wished him well and said I would keep him in my prayers. He thanked me, and said, "You know, Father, after my heart first went wacky years ago, the doctors said they couldn't do much beyond what they were already doing. I was shaken by this, but I gradually came to a realization: I believe in God. And whether I stand here alive in this world or die and enter into the next, I am in the hands of God. I'm not perfect, but I know God loves me, forgives me, and cares for me. And knowing that, I feel a peace that has stayed with me ever since. I can enjoy life all the better now, no matter what happens."

Good man! Realistic man! I knew I was standing face-to-face with a person of faith. Faith isn't just for good days. It's especially for the bad days. We all worry so much about so many things. We worry so often that we rob ourself of spontaneity and life. We claim we believe in a God, but Max Lucado reminds us of reality:

> Still we worry. We worry about the IRS and the SAT and the FBI. We worry about education, recreation, and constipation. We worry that we won't have enough money, and when we have money we worry that we won't manage it well. We worry that the world will end before the parking meter expires. We worry what the dog thinks if he sees us step out of the shower. We worry that someday we'll learn that fat-free yogurt was fattening.

Then Lucado asks a pointed question: "Honestly, now. Did God save you so you would fret?"

Believing in the spiritual aspect of existence is an ongoing endeavor. Though faith is a gift, we dispose ourself for that gift by asking for it, by training our eyes and heart to look beyond the horizon to see through the dark times. Believing is countercultural because culture demands that we believe that this—the material world—is all there is.

If we base our life on what secular culture teaches, we experience more stress, fear, and restlessness. The results of living a solid spiritual life are evident in the man with the bad heart—inner peace, trust, less worry, the ability to better enjoy this world.

How can we get to this point? Each journey of faith is unique, so we have no set formula. We have to struggle at it. We need to pray daily, even if we wonder if there's a God to hear our prayer. We must talk to God from our heart—and listen. When two people hope to grow in a relationship, they must commit themselves to communicate often and well. We can converse with God when driving alone, walking alone, exercising alone, resting in bed alone, or sitting alone in our favorite chair.

Reading and reflecting on solid books, listening to good preaching, engaging in substantive discussions with realistic, levelheaded people, worshiping at church or temple, and living life enthusiastically are additional ways to grow spiritually. Suffering and silence, though we often seek to avoid both, also have the power to open us to belief.

A sad lie permeates the world—that God is a bore and that spirituality is opposed to sexuality and causes a loss of personal freedom and good times. To make a case against such thinking, I'd present as exhibit A all the people like my friend with the arrhythmic heart. Those people see the larger, truer view of life that many others have missed.

When a Child Dies

WHEN A CHILD DIES, we are left without answers. Such a tragic event is extremely painful and impossible to understand, especially for the child's parents. Feelings of injustice, anger, sorrow, and confusion envelop us. Through tears we ask the most common question of life—why?

In an attempt to answer this cry, some offer the sentiments expressed in tender poems and condolences that claim that sometimes "God calls little children to dwell with him above." Or, "Perhaps God tires of calling the aged in His fold, so He picks a rosebud before it can grow old; God knows how much we need them so He takes but few, to make the land of heaven more beautiful to view."

While well-meaning, such "answers" have very distressing implications. At precisely the time that parents need to be assured of God's compassion, God is named as the cause of their pain. Many theologians and clergy shudder at such "explanations" for tragedies because they paint images of God that are contrary to the image of God in the Scriptures.

Our image of God is extremely important to our spiritual and religious life. Our practice of religion will suffer if our image of God is inadequate. We already have an unhelpful tendency to consider God as nothing more than an enlarged picture of childhood authority figures. Images of a God who arbitrarily takes children away from their parents are also unhelpful and irresponsible. Shall we forget all the scriptural images of the God who heals and feeds and raises us up? Of the God who unites and brings together?

So what can we think when we are faced with the tragic death of a child? We look for cause and effect, reasons and explanations, someone to blame. Why does a criminal live to be ninety while an innocent child dies so young? We live our lives surrounded by the mystery of suffering, not always understanding—just as Job could not—the answer to it all.

If there is an answer, it is found in acknowledging our inability to understand, yet to eventually summon faith and trust in the One who transcends us. If we take the Scriptures seriously, we can trust a God who is close and loving, a God who can write straight with crooked lines. Process theology claims that God feels our pain along with us and grieves. At Christmastime do we not call him Emmanuel, God-with-us?

In our mind we usually have difficulty exonerating God from being the cause of tragedies. The friends of Job had a similar image of God. Their explanations for Job's suffering can be summarized as, "God did this to you." But when Jesus' contemporaries asked him if a man's blindness was the result of a hidden sin of the man or his parents, Jesus quickly replied, "Neither!" We find it so hard to accept that this is an imperfect world. Life is sometimes secure and predictable, sometimes random, chaotic, and unexplainable. We would like to understand and control it, but we can't. What is within our ability is to despair—or to believe and to trust.

People of faith believe that in the beginning of what we call time, an inscrutable God took chaotic darkness and brought out of it life, order, and beauty. People of faith keep believing, even when caught in the mad whirl of chaotic darkness, that this same God will eventually bring life, order, and beauty out of it for us. People of faith believe that in some paradoxical way, a child who dies early will experience no disadvantage whatsoever in the timeless life that follows. We can only entrust our lost children to God, and say in the words of Anne Porter,

> To take the place of the child
> Isaac there was a ram
> But for all those others
> There was no ram
>   And I lay down all these deaths
> I lay them down at your feet
> So that you can keep them for me
> Since by myself
> I am unable
> To understand them.

Are
We
Plugged
In
to
Quality?

AS WE GROW FARTHER APART, we try to connect more. For a nation with more than its share of broken homes, racial distance, and fragile relationships, we are caught up in a whirl of communication technology. Hyper-communication is in. We're all supposed to have a cellular phone, call waiting, a fax machine, a beeper, a modem, an answering machine, e-mail, voice mail, and Internet service. To most of us, not one of those things has special meaning; technology is simply meeting our business needs. Some of us look deeper and wonder why we have this urge to be plugged in to everyone everywhere.

Psychologist James Hillman suggests that we are addicted to communication today because we are lonely and seek proof of our worthwhile existence. Playing on Descartes's principle, "I think, therefore, I am," Hillman says that today's method of proof is, "I am because I am accessible." This fact unconsciously demonstrates that in a busy but lonely world, others know we are here. If we didn't matter, would they be trying to contact us? Yet we can legitimately wonder, Is the vast network of communication instruments putting an end to our aloneness? Unlikely.

No matter how sophisticated our instruments of communication become, the human heart always waits for the same messages. We wait to be affirmed by another person, to know that we are understood, appreciated, and genuinely loved. All the communication technology in the world will never substitute for the quality we seek.

The core, or heart, of a human person is immeasurably deep. We spend our life hoping our deepness and another's deepness will connect personally and authentically. We hope another heart will choose to come down vertically into the depths of our heart and know us, and allow us to know it in return. If this vertical type of authentic intimacy fades, if deeps stop answering deeps, then horizontal communication intensifies—beeps answer beeps—as a shallow substitute.

Humans will always hunger for solid relationships, closeness, intimacy—for deeps answering deeps. Communication is essential in achieving this, but the jabber of horizontal communication that merely skips across the surface of life is not. We need a deeper communication that goes beyond our being accessible for an agenda filled with business, sports, politics, gossip, or the weather.

Achieving heart-to-heart communication requires far more than becoming plugged in electronically or transmitting messages via satellite or fiber optics. Heart-to-heart communication begins with the person trying to communicate. We must first and foremost come to know ourself. To do this we must occasionally unplug ourself from the network of wall-to-wall words, and not fear silent solitude. *Not* being accessible to everyone else permits us to become more accessible to ourself. The truth about intimate relationships is that they can never be any better than our relationship with ourself. And as we come to know ourself, we must undertake the risk of communicating the reality of ourself to another, and that other person must be willing to take the same risk with us. This requires much quality time together, much work, much willingness to be open and to understand.

Communication addiction only looks like communication. Getting lost in the chitter-chatter of the world can work against real communication with a real person. A man who comes home from work, eats, corrects the kids' behavior, watches the news, then goes to his computer and surfs the Web for hours every night, may deem himself a good communicator, a man who is really in touch. After all, doesn't he "communicate" with his office and the whole world on the Web? Yet later that night he may wonder why his wife is sexually unresponsive. Sexuality is one of the greatest channels for the interaction of human hearts. If his heart doesn't communicate with his wife's heart, why does he think her body will communicate with his?

What is it that we want to hear above all the beeps, hums, rings, and clicking of our amazing technology? We want to hear what humans have always wanted to hear—that we are understood, appreciated, and truly loved. Multiplying the medium must never supplant the message.

Our Contract with the Universe

WE PRESUME THAT WE HAVE an unspoken contract with the universe—that if we are good at heart, try hard, and act right, things will work out well for us. We could call it a mutual reciprocity with life. If we do our part, life will do its part; if we scratch its back, it will scratch ours—a pragmatic fairness. Nobody has specifically told us about this contract. We just presume it exists.

When life doesn't seem to keep its part of the contract, we complain and become angry. "I've tried to live a pretty decent life, so why did I get nothing but sickness and problems this past year?" a man complains. "She's had it so easy all her life and has so much; I've worked hard and have so little," sighs a woman.

An objective consideration of contemporary life and human history painfully teaches us that no such contract exists. But what made us ever think that life signed such a contract with us? One influence is the sense of justice that lives in our conscience and likely was fostered by our parents and teachers. Justice speaks to us correctly of fairness, and ought to be our constant guide of behavior. We erroneously conclude, however, that full justice is always accomplished in this world. The various religions of the world and our own Scriptures convincingly show us that the inequities of life are not always settled here on earth. The life beyond this life is where complete justice and mercy occur.

Another influence is our ego, the controlling part of our personality. Through it we seek a certain godlike control over life. We want to be assured that if we do A, B will result; if we are kind, people will be kind to us. We want to control life to make favorable

21

things happen to us and to avoid the unfavorable. We want to have the security of knowing that if we work hard for a company all our life, the company will never lay us off. If, despite our best efforts, unfairness bites us in the backside, we are angered and disappointed. Nietzsche once noted how dismayed we become when we discover that we are not God and that we don't control the universe.

When we are young, our illusion of control remains strong. Until adolescence ends—some psychologists say that's at about the age of twenty-five, or later, in our society—we continue to believe we are gods. But during midlife and thereafter, the sad news is gradually announced—and eventually shouted—to us: Life is not always fair! You are not God, but merely a mortal creature! You don't have the control you think you do!

Midlife humbles us. It doesn't want to defeat us, but it wants to show us reality and encourage us to accept it. Fairness and justice are noble goals, and we are not to abandon them, but their fullest expression will never be found here. Our attempts at godlike control are understandable, but after doing our best, we must eventually surrender to God the things that are God's.

Experience unsparingly asks us to grow up, to meet reality, and to take responsibility for our life. Rather than deflect or control experience by way of our illusory contract with the universe, we must confront our humanness with all its weaknesses, dependencies, complexities, and fears. That means we must stop blaming others, including God, for our lot in life; we must take responsibility for our physical, emotional, and spiritual well-being. That means we must stop playing control games with life or with others, and face ourself. There is a great spiritual component to life. When we find ourself in a world of unfairness and our control grows ineffectual, it is then we become ripe for discovering our true self and God.

If we could make a contract with the universe, if we could control every aspect of our life and avoid all problems and injustices, what would we become? If we were never humbled, would we learn who we really are? If our heart never hurt and unfairness never conquered, would we learn compassion and acceptance? If we lived a whole life thinking we were God, would we ever find the one who is?

Being in Control

ONE OF OUR MORE DANGEROUS desires is our desire to always be in control. That desire is dangerous because it implies that humans are like machines or computers, and that life is part of a manageable technology. Cars have steering wheels and brakes that help us maintain control. Our furnace and air conditioner have controls that allow us to adjust our personal climate to suit us. Everything operable has control buttons and levers.

We seek to control our careers by taking the right courses in college. We seek to control our business deals by making the right contacts. We seek to control our game of golf by taking more lessons. We try to control our friends, our spouse, and our children by various manipulations. We seek to control our health and longevity by diet and exercise. We even try to control God. We look for a never-fail prayer, or we point to good behavior that will make God answer and give us what we ask, or make happen what we want to happen. Our fond hope is to be in control of life itself.

When is our life deemed out of control? When we have an accident, get fired, suffer, develop a serious illness, become overwhelmed at work, life seems out of control. When we crumble financially, experience the death of a loved one, endure a natural disaster, or notice ourself aging, life seems out of control.

We can feel out of control when positive things happen as well—the head rush of feelings when we are infatuated or falling in love, when we win the lottery, when we get an unexpected promotion, when we survive a brush with death, or when we witness the birth of a long-awaited child.

23

Those positive and negative situations are the warp and woof of life. Life is a combination of losing and finding, of succeeding and failing, of being heartbroken and heartfilled. Too much emphasis on control might mean that we are trying to suppress the mystery.

Older people who have lived a full life have many stories to tell, stories that cause laughter and tears when they tell them. Their stories recount many of the times when they were not in control—surviving the storm by hiding in the basement, experiencing the broken hearts on the way to true love. But they now seem to be glad to have gone through all that and survived. These experiences have made their life rich and colorful, stretching them into fuller persons. So it seems that on one level we want to be out of control and in the hands of mystery, and on another level we are fighting to be in control. That is what people do. That is our dilemma.

We need a certain spiritual maturity to realize that we are not in control, that we do not have all the answers, or the power, to carry out our plans all the time. The sheer truth of our powerlessness leads us toward a certain "emptying out," or surrender. Not a surrender of despair, but a willingness to hand over our lives to a greater Being who loves us and is in perfect control. Many traditions call this being God, and the subtle control God exercises over our life is called Providence. We trust God to ultimately bring us through the uncontrollable aspects of life, not because we deserve it but because God loves us. God controls things so thoroughly and mysteriously that order, beauty, and peace enter into our tenuous lives. At times when we feel we have lost our grip on the wheel, that is good to know.

The Ebb and Flow of Life

WHO DOES NOT SENSE a movement in his or her life? Who has not felt the strong flow of a wonderful tide at one time, and its ebbing away at another? Why must we be bothered with fluctuations and changes?

Seasonal affective disorders, hormones, warm or cold weather, rainy days or sunshine, something we ate, the children's behavior—all are possible reasons for such changes. Beyond these reasons, however, there is much more.

Like it or not, we must acknowledge the element of mystery in our life. There is something unknown that shows itself and at the same time withdraws. We know it's there, but we know we cannot grasp it or command it. We experience it in the coming and going of time, in erratic cycles, in our ups and downs, even in the midst of our relationships and work. It hints at mystery.

Mysterious and great things, beautiful and sweet things always seem to ebb and flow. Mystery never acts as we think it should. That is what makes it mystery. It is beyond our taking in; it shows itself, then pulls back, lest it overpower.

Our daily lives ebb and flow, as does love, as does faith. Sometimes our love flows strong. At other times it ebbs, and we question it. Even our spirituality is not spared the ebb and flow of mystery. Conviction gives way to doubt, then doubt to conviction.

That ebb and flow frightens us. Our egos want to hold tight to certainty and security. Comings and goings are unsettling; we yearn for certitude—so much so that even in our religions, where we seek contact with the mysterious One, dogmatism is often more highly valued than mystery.

The same is true in human relationships. When we draw close to another, we rarely think of approaching mystery. We expect predictability. We expect our relationships to never waver, emotions to be always pleasant and warm, and our understanding of one another complete. When the mystery of love ebbs, we question the relationship rather than enter the mystery that invites us in.

Instead of certitude, security, and predictability, we keep coming face-to-face with mystery in this world. Mystery flirts with us. Like an unpretentious and beautiful woman, mystery shows enough of herself to intrigue us, then draws back. In the times of her presence, we believe we have finally won her heart forever. But then her presence ebbs away. We feel hopeless, doubting we'll ever see her again. Yet her memory entices us to seek her once again.

That ebbing and flowing, that going and coming, is not meant to make us distrust life, or love, or God; it is meant to lead us along a road. As we chase the mystery—*if* we chase the mystery—we achieve a sense of going somewhere we've never been but are destined to go. It's not forbidden territory but rarefied territory. We sense that we're progressing in an awesome endeavor that is greater than ourself. We are traveling on a road that goes on forever. On and on. If we look back, we know we have traveled far already. If we look ahead, past the turn in the road and over the hill, we'll sense that we still stand on only the threshold of mystery. To those truly alive, there burns a desire to move on—whatever it takes. Ahead is where good lives and where healthy relationships and vibrant faith are forged.

Security, routine, and comfort continuously urge us to demystify life and love and faith. If we follow that road, living, loving, and believing become small and trifling. Sad will be the day when we conclude that we have figured out the greatest mysteries of life. We need mystery more than we need bread. Yet mystery will always ebb and flow. It cannot do otherwise, or else it is not mystery. Most Rev. Fulton J. Sheen aptly writes:

> There comes a moment in even the noblest of human loves when the mystery has gone. One has now grown "used to" the best, and has come to take it for granted, as jewelers may casually handle the most precious stones without troubling to admire them. What we completely possess, we can no longer desire. What we have already attained, we cannot hope for. Yet hope and desire and, above all, mystery are needed to keep our interest in life alive.

Fully Known, Fully Loved

CAN YOU LOVE a pet cat you never had? Can you love salmon if you have never tasted it? Can someone be your favorite teacher if you have never had her or him as a teacher?

The human mind is divided into intellect and will. Our intellect knows and judges, our will chooses and seeks. When we experience something new, our intellect acts first. It seeks to understand and know the object, experience, or person, and to determine whether it is good for us. If our intellect judges a new thing as distasteful to us in some way, our will rejects it. If our intellect finds the knowledge of the new thing good for us in some way, then our will chooses it. Sometimes we use the word *love* to express a judgment we have made, as when we say, "I love french fries," which means "I choose french fries because I enjoy how they taste." If we meet a person whom our intellect judges as good, then our will chooses that person as a potential friend or lover. Our will seeks what our intellect judges as good.

Knowledge comes before love. That's why we can't love a cat we never knew, or the taste of salmon we have never eaten, or a teacher we never had in class. That is also why there is no such thing as love at first sight. We can feel attraction at first sight, infatuation at first sight, or desire at first sight, but we cannot love at first sight. Our intellect has to get to know someone well before our will can make that deep, intimate choice to love that person.

To really come to love someone, then, requires that we come to know that person. Suppose you are a man sitting in a room, and I say to you: "There is a woman outside in the hall whom I'd like you to meet. She is

27

extremely beautiful, intelligent, charming, and promises to be completely devoted to whomever she loves. The moment you meet her, you will love her more deeply than you've ever loved anyone before."

What a claim! But it's not possible. You may feel infatuated or desirous of her or find her most beautiful, but you're not ready to love her fully. For suppose she truly is beautiful, but you come to know that she is also conceited. She is intelligent, but you come to know that she is unable to communicate honestly with you. She is charming, but you come to know that she is unforgiving and vindictive. She wants to be completely devoted to whomever she loves, but you come to know that she is still too immature to love you or anyone. Those are all crucial facets of personality that we can only learn about in time, not at first sight, no matter how stirring. The kind of intimate love the human heart seeks develops gradually, as you come to know the whole person.

The words *intellect* and *will* may sound cold and mechanical, but they serve to remind us that for genuine, satisfying relationships, communication is the key. Unless a person knows us fully or to a significant degree, that person cannot fully or significantly love us. We must take the risk of revealing ourself as honestly as possible.

Most of us spend our life hiding. We hide so that we *won't* be known. Revealing ourself to others entails the great risks of being rejected or disregarded. So we put our best face forward, the parts of ourself we are confident will be accepted and approved. The rest we try to hide. We are willing to let others see our strengths but not our vulnerability. We are willing to let others see some of our anger but not our tenderness or neediness.

If we live that way, no one will ever fully know our whole real self, and we may never be loved the way we yearn to be. Just as someone cannot fully enjoy a movie if four-fifths of the screen is blocked, someone cannot fully love another if that other never reveals her or his true self.

To cross over from the land of tepid love to the land of intimate love, we must cross the bridge of risk, communicating as we go. There is no other way. As we reveal ourself to another, wonderful things happen—our fears turn into trust, our inadequacies are accepted.

The Languages of God

ALL RELIGIONS URGE PEOPLE to pray. Most of us admit to the need of prayer as a matter of principle, but we don't always follow through in practice. Perhaps prayer seems too difficult, too futile, too time consuming. We're busy and easily distracted, so we give up on the idea. We leave prayer for monks, clergy, and those threatened by some calamity.

One of the reasons we find prayer difficult is that we have a narrow understanding of what prayer means. We conclude that prayer always means *saying* something—most likely in formalized or high-sounding language. We're more inclined to speak to God than to listen to God. We want to tell God how to make our life happy, safe, or secure. Our main frustration about prayer is that God never seems to be around to listen to us. We imagine that God is focused on the tragedy of someone starving in a distant land or someone dying in a hospital bed. Our second frustration is that God never says anything to us, so we find it difficult to listen. "Speak, Lord, your servant is listening," we'd like to call out many times.

It is quite an awakening, however, to realize how focused on us God really is. God is constantly speaking to us. We are unaware of the many languages of God. God's most special communication to us, of course, is in the Scriptures. Humans wrote the words, but God inspired them.

But words are just one way of communicating. God finds many ways, other than with human words, to speak to us. Like a radio with only one station setting, we don't tune in to the countless stations on different wavelengths. Sometimes God speaks in the language of conscience, which lives in the core of our heart. God speaks through the voice of our duties and responsibilities, urging us to know them and carry them out. God speaks in the language of beauty, the most visual of all languages. If we are open enough, God speaks in the language of suffering, too, which is a universal language that is capable of communicating things that no other can. Our psyche as well, with its inexorable push toward wholeness, is the personal place where God whispers and directs us toward becoming the human we were created to be.

One essential condition for listening to God is silence. We must learn to be still and listen. The world is afraid of silence. We carry, wherever we go, electronic devices that play music or keep us otherwise connected. We give many reasons for being so accessible to others and keeping ourself entertained. But more likely, the real reason is that silence is scary. We are frightened to be so utterly with our self. Silence draws us to our depths, and that is where we find our true self and God. That's the place where we and God communicate the most. And we're afraid of what we might hear.

Just as we sometimes fear intimacy with another human, we're especially afraid of intimacy with God. "I was afraid, because I was naked; and I hid myself" (Genesis 3:10). We fear being seen as we truly are, because we are imperfect. We think imperfection means rejection, so we hide behind chatter, words, busyness, and illusions.

To learn how to pray well and to listen to the language of God can be the most freeing experience in the world. Despite our imperfection and sin, God continues to call us from our hiding places and fears, to meet and experience Love. We will never know that unless we allow God to tell us in God's own language.

Love and Forgive

THE FUNERAL WAS OVER. My family and I were at the home of a friend whose husband had died in a car accident. She remarked, "He was a great guy, and we got along fine; I don't remember us ever having an argument." Listeners smiled approvingly, slowly shaking their heads at the tragic termination of such an ideal relationship, perhaps even feeling a tinge of envy.

My feelings were on a different track. Sure, I had always thought of them as a good couple and good people. I still do. But when I heard the widow's boast, I wondered how close they *really* had been. Can two individuals really live for long in an intimate relationship and never have some differences or misunderstandings? We all would like relationships to be this way. In fact, we used to think they were this way and always ended our stories with, "They married and lived happily ever after."

In reality romance and confrontation are linked. Nothing carries more potential for satisfaction—or for hurt and disappointment —than a long-term relationship like marriage. We bring to our relationships a great deal of hope and need, as well as a deep capacity for either fulfilling growth or petrifaction.

Two healthy people—if they maintain a sense of self and individuality—are bound to have occasional disagreements and disappointments. For the sake of our own growth and our relationship, we *need* to experience occasional differences. Disagreements, handled in a mature way, facilitate humility and genuine communication, compromise and understanding. Living together on a daily basis relentlessly wears away our projections and illusions. We eventually come to see more clearly who we really are and who the one we love really is.

Human growth usually occurs in relationships, not in isolation. Relationships help us to see our sharp edges, to develop sensitivity, and to continue discovering how to better love and forgive. Where we are deficient, relationships call us to do something about it.

"You're not the person I married," one spouse often laments to the other. Actually a spouse never is. A spouse is a stranger we barely knew, and now we know that person a little better. The satisfaction of relationships comes from mending disagreements, communicating our true selves, and proceeding together on the road of acceptance and love. That is how the richness and texture of deepening relationships occur. Too many of us expect a good relationship to come easily and to leave easily when it doesn't work out. An old French adage proclaims that only the beginning of love is beautiful. We'd call that the honeymoon stage. Some prefer to stay there, but rarely does this happen.

Relationships are the meat of life. If a life passes without them, we have to wonder what it was all about. That is why relationships are worth all the effort we can muster to preserve and mend them. John Shea says it well:

> A long-lasting relationship is made up of a thousand breaks and a thousand mendings.
>
> Paradoxically, this process of breaking and mending does not make the bond weaker but stronger. The reason is that we can begin to understand our part in how things break and in how things mend. Most of us never get good enough to prevent the breaks, but most of us do get inventive and creative enough to pursue the mending. The key to mending is to think not that you are putting something back together again but that you are creating something completely new out of what broke. It is not a matter of going back. It is a matter of going forward, of integrating events into larger and larger wholes.

The art of creating an "us" out of two "I's" is slowly being forgotten. Pieces of disagreements and fragile egos lie all around on the ground. We need to learn how to pick up the pieces and put them together, creating a beautiful new mosaic.

The
Art
of
Surrender

IT IS NOT EASY to surrender. Most of the time we are trying to win, to stay in control, to run things. Without even thinking about them, our egos are constantly striving for these purposes. We are eager to defend ourself from being perceived as weak, wounded, needy, or not in control. When our stomach growls in a crowd, we feel slightly embarrassed—not so much by the natural sound as by having no control over it. We think, "I should at least be able to control the sounds of my own body."

When two road-rage combatants are dueling in their cars, who wants to back off and surrender? In order to stay in control and look strong and sufficient, we make our way through life using gruff language, power plays, and assertive manipulations. Who wants to surrender? Surrender means only one thing— weakness.

But there are two kinds of surrender, and sometimes surrender is a sign of strength or wisdom. Surrendering at the right time is an art. Surrendering simply to give up is unhealthy and unartistic. This type of surrender demonstrates a lack of personal courage or a desire to be taken care of by someone else. It betrays a desire for life to be easy. People who have talents but give up using them out of fear of failure or fear of the effort required, people who give up working through hard times because the struggle demands too much, and people who surrender responsibility for their children because it disturbs their comfort are unhealthy surrenderers. Such surrender indicates weakness of character, a soft self.

The artistic form of surrender, however, requires great courage, honesty, and humility. We accede to reality, to another, or to God

33

out of love. We gracefully give in when we really can't do what is asked of us. Those who accept the limitations of body or mind without seeing themselves as a victim, those who accept failure even though they've tried their best, and those who can swallow their pride and say, "I was wrong, you were right," demonstrate the art of surrender. The art of surrender is perhaps most clearly seen in those who set aside their earnest prayers and surrender to God and say, "Whatever *you* want!" Surrender opens us up but leaves our integrity intact. In fact, surrender increases our integrity.

To learn the healthy art of surrender, we must peel off any self-interested desires and break through our own will for the sake of another's. The healthy art of surrender requires an understanding of paradox —that when we seem to give up, we receive; when we appear weak, we are strong.

The art of surrender eventually brings us face-to-face with God. In our final act of surrender, we are impelled to cry out with astounding realization, "All that I thought I lost, I found in God's arms."

A Tribute to Trees

YOU WERE SO BEAUTIFUL this year. Of course you have never disappointed us no matter how muted you dress. For several weeks your presence is as unavoidable as perfumed air. You envelop us, and we are seduced by you on hillsides and country lanes. Some of us—those with good noses and ears—don't need to see you to love you. We could walk blindfolded down neighborhood streets or through parks and still know you are here. You whisper in rustling breezes. In the darkest of nights, we can hear your leaves fall, swirl in the wind, or crunch underfoot. You do something to us. Your wild, ripe aromas touch special spots in us. You stir the nostalgia of long-gone times, you slow down our pace, you call out to us, "Oh, look up, look around, don't keep looking down."

We wait for your magnificent parade each year—a parade in which you stand still while we move and run from place to place to see you as we pass. And we enjoy the parade! For trees teach us something about virtue and beauty all year round. They portray what they teach. For years they loyally stand by us as teachers and inconspicuous friends. They show us that a living thing can exist for years, take all that life dishes out, and survive. They offer us the lesson that we can do that too. Stand by a tree, touch its rough bark, and notice its gnarly branches. Think of all the years it has stood there growing and living. Think of all it has seen, all that tried and tested it. It has endured heat and parched earth, ice storms, heavy rains and wild winds, infestation and broken limbs, yet it is alive and strong. Its inner rings indelibly mark its commitment to life. Trees exhibit such a steady character and stability that we are often sad when old trees are felled, whether by human or natural act. Trees are trustworthy teachers.

Autumn is glory time for trees. If they wanted to boast, they could surely do it then. Yet they are humble in their best times. Their appearance is enhanced by the quiet dignity they maintain. True beauty is always unassuming, waiting for us to notice.

Trees teach us that there are all kinds of beauty. In springtime, when they stretch their arms in the balmy winds, shudder to the passion of new life, and grow to more than they were before, they call us to come along with them. They bid us to grow more beautiful, to become new and free again. In summer they teach us the beauty of service to others. They give shade from the wearying sunlight to all who seek it; they offer their branches for the play of children or for nests of birds; they breathe forth life-giving oxygen, sustaining other organisms. Trees teach us the beauty of caring for others.

In winter, when the fulsome clothes of leaves they wore are all swept up or gone down into the earth, another beauty is noticed in the trees. Denuded, they stand before us with a serene simplicity, not a self-conscious shame. They are willing to be authentic, to be seen just as they are. We seldom see ourself that way, nor permit others to see us that way. We work hard at maintaining our covers—our defenses and personas—all year round, all our life. Trees teach us the spiritual beauty of unadorned simplicity and unposed authenticity. They bid us look inward, know ourself, and be who we are.

In winter go for walks in the dark of evening. The summer sounds of earth are hushed, and the shuffling race of life walks softer in many places. There's only the bark of a dog in the distance. Look up at the trees—they always bid us look up, not down. Encouraging, they are. Even in the austerity imposed by winter, trees are a beauty to behold. In the stark simplicity of black and white, their branches form an irregular lacework against the sky, especially when the moon shines through them. Trees teach us their best lesson on those nights. They remind us that beneath all our efforts to hide, to be busy, to look better, to seem successful, or to compare ourself to others, we possess a mighty dignity and beauty in just being who we are.

Truth— What's That?

AMERICA AND ITS PEOPLE are having trouble with the truth these days. Once again we're acting like sheeple. Sheeple are people who are easily led, easily fooled. Sheeple feed on little pieces of opinion or self-interest that sound clever but are junk food when compared to truth.

We nibble on so much that we may wonder if there is anything called truth, whether some values are always true, no matter how old they are or how glossed over they become. We have always struggled with truth. Centuries ago a Roman politician named Pontius Pilate walked onto a sunlit portico and washed his hands of honesty while he cynically asked, "What is truth?" Cleverness and polls now substitute for truth. Truth now seems to be whatever we want it to be.

Who Needs God? asks the title of one of Rabbi Harold Kushner's books. He reminds us that the source of truth is God. He relates a discussion with some of his students about the Holocaust and Hitler's good-sounding "truths" about Jewish inferiority. After considering the laws Hitler passed to sanction his actions against the Jews, to make those actions legal, Kushner asked, "Why was Hitler wrong?" "What do you mean, why was Hitler wrong?" one student asked. "Do you mean he may have been right?" Someone else said, "You can't just take people and kill them because you don't like them." Kushner asked: "Are you trying to tell me that some things are wrong even if a majority of the people think they are right? Are you telling me that there is such a thing as right and wrong built into the human conscience, and it's not just a matter of how you feel about it?" After some silence, a student answered: "Well, yeah, I guess so. I never thought about it that way before."

That student has a lot of company. Many people seem not to think about the nature of truth. "What's truth?" they ask. Lawyers, politicians, advertisers, press agents, spin doctors—they all play fast and loose with the truth. If someone can lie and win a court case, lie and sell a product, lie and get off the hook, what's wrong with that? What's truth? Yet to live in a society or in a home, to develop solid personal relationships or work together as colleagues, to run a business, or to buy or sell a car, truth is essential. Without truth a society will gradually fall apart. What's truth? If we don't know, we better learn. We need it badly.

The practice of lying is not new in our society. Humans have always lied. What is new is the loss of belief that truth exists. If there is no objective truth, if all reasoning and behavior is our own rationalizing, then we are slowly losing our way. The distinction between lying and telling the truth presupposes that truth exists—that there is an objective truth from which we stray when we lie. Objective truth is truth that is so, has been so, and will always be so, regardless of the century in which we live. Many today have abandoned the belief in objective truth.

What's truth? Why are some things true? If there is a God who demands moral behavior, then there is truth and error, good and evil. We are not the determiners of truth—God is. Kushner says:

> The assertion that there is only one God is the assertion that issues of moral behavior are not matters of personal taste. We cannot decide by majority vote that it is all right to steal and lie, any more than we can decide that winters should be mild or cookies more nourishing than vegetables.

So how do we answer our, or Pilate's, question, "What is truth?" The definition I learned in philosophy class has been used for centuries. *Veritas est adequatio rei et intellectus:* "Truth is an equalness between my intellect and reality." Reality comes from God, who made everything out of nothing, according to God's own intention and plan. When our intellect is in sync with what God wants, says, and expects of creation, then we possess the truth. When we are out of sync, we are wrong. In the brightness of God's truth and our weakness in grasping it, we will be judged fairly and understandingly. But let us never think we can either ignore it—not seek it—or live happily without it.

38

Dealing with Our Wounds

PHOTOGRAPHS CAN BE digitally altered or airbrushed to remove minor blemishes or scars. Would that we could do that to our psyche. The word *psyche* comes from the Greek word meaning "soul," and stands for the inner core of our person. If our personal psyche could be photographed, it would need much altering, for each of us has scars, each of us has been wounded in life.

We all have wounds because we all have a life history. Birth itself is a kind of gigantic wound. After that we can be wounded in many ways: by treatment that is too harsh or too soft; by dysfunctional behavior; by parents who remain too coldly distant and nonempathetic, or who suffocate us with too much attention and control. Wounds can be caused by poverty, affluence, sexuality, neglect, violence, loneliness, abandonment, and by a thousand and one other factors of life. No one has perfect parents or utopian childhoods, so no one escapes the infliction of wounds.

Even when dormant and covered with a scar, wounds affect our life. They can surface in certain situations. For example, a person who felt suffocated by rigidity and control as a child can experience anxiety as an adult when someone deals with him or her in a very controlling or rigid way. Some people, wounded by perfectionistic demands of parents, might find their wounds opened by others or by their own inner compulsions. They feel they must constantly meet others' expectations. They can't say no, and they have difficulty relaxing and forgetting impending duties. Their wounds lead them to be their own harsh critic.

When our wounds are opened by some event, we usually experience anxiety in our life. Therefore, the more we know about our wounds and their origins, the more we can cope with the anxieties and fears that come from them. The wounds of our psyche are similar to the wounds of our body. If someone touches a wound on our body, we hurt, and at the same time remember the occasion of the wound. The same goes for the wounds in our psyche. When one of them is disturbed, we hurt. We experience discomfort reminiscent of the initial wounding.

An example of a life-affecting wound occurred in the formation of a phobia in a woman I'll call Ceil. Ceil had a severe fear of moths. As an adult she was extremely agitated whenever a moth appeared. After a period of analysis, Ceil discovered the cause of her phobia.

When Ceil was in elementary school, she learned that her mother was pregnant. She was invited to feel the movement of the child. Relatives awaited the new baby with excitement. Not Ceil, however. Suffering the pangs of impending dethronement, she quietly hated the baby. During the pregnancy Ceil was studying insects at school. One of the insects she studied was the moth. It burrowed into dark places and destroyed clothes by eating them. In Ceil's childish imagination, she wished she could momentarily be a moth, burrow through her mother's belly button, and destroy the new baby everyone awaited. This wish brought with it much anger and guilt. She feared disaster if her wish was ever discovered.

When the baby was born, Ceil forgot her awful death wish against her brother. They grew up to be playmates and friends. But she remained extremely frightened of moths. Her fear seemed irrational to her and to others until she was finally able to revisit the original feelings and desires that formed it. She was able to acknowledge her wound, which came from the fear of being dethroned, unloved, and rejected in favor of a new child, combined with the unresolved guilt that came from the evil wish to kill her brother.

Our wounds cannot be airbrushed away. We must come to know them and understand why and how they were formed. If we can't do that on our own, we can obtain the help of a competent psychologist or psychiatrist—whatever it takes. Knowing our wounds permits us to deal with them as the adults we are now, not as the impotent children we were when we suffered them.

Believing in a Personal God

WE SEE CONSTANT REMINDERS of how many people are living today. Teeming foreign countries, crowded streets, jammed sports stadiums, and interstate traffic all glide by before our eyes. A million here, a billion there. It's easy to feel insignificant and lost in the masses.

What are we to think when we hear statements claiming the opposite? "Are not five sparrows sold for two pennies? Yet not one of them is forgotten in God's sight. But even the hairs of your head are all counted. Do not be afraid; you are of more value than many sparrows" (Luke 12:6–7). In the midst of so many people, do I count that much? Am I not lost in a blurred vision God has of the billions who breathe along with me right now? There are so many needs, so much pain, so many claims on the attention of God. How can God be concerned with my loneliness when someone else is dying of hunger?

When parents look into a crowded school yard, whom do they see? Don't they look for their child? Is it childish dreaming to imagine that God, looking at this world, sometimes looks to see just me? Can I even imagine that God's attention lingers on me for more than a minute, a second? It seems too much to imagine that God constantly looks upon me with affection. I discount that possibility because of my averageness, my sins, and the illogical idea that God fully thinks of two people at once, much less billions at a time. Yet that is my secret hope. And in some grand mysterious way, that is what happens. We all are in God's thoughts all the time.

"Impossible," we say. "Contradictory." And if God were like us, we would be correct. But God is not like us. God is transcendent.

41

God's essence goes beyond and above and over everything else. God is, as a theologian says, the "One Utterly Beyond" the stretches of our imagination. Because we always look out from our inner world through human eyes, we expect only the human to happen. We seldom consider God's incomprehensibility.

God can look at billions of people, collectively and individually, at the same time. God sees me, each one of us, as the only one. God sees me with such thoroughness and love that I would be overwhelmed if I realized it.

When I can let God be God, the One beyond the limitations humanness sets, I am consoled. To know that I am in God's constant thought, that I am the child he looks for as he gazes at the school yard of life, is a confounding realization. In one way I run from that truth because I fear it places too heavy a burden on me, weak as I am. But when I understand that being the apple of God's eye flows from his unconditional love and doesn't depend on what I do or accomplish, or how weak I am, then my awe is intensified. God is a personal God because God is God, and God created me. The thought of me was lovable to God.

To live with increasing awareness of God's understanding and loving attention is to live with increasing inner peace. Too often, however, we are educated about God in the same way as some third-grade children I visited many years ago. I asked them, "What does God do all day?" There was a flurry of hands, and the student I selected said, "He's watching us." "Why?" I inquired. "To see if we do anything wrong," came the reply. How sad. Today I wonder, Did that child grow up to be an adult who has a fearful awkwardness of being in God's eye?

God is a personal God who is more interested in each of us than we can fathom. The trivial occurrences as well as the critical elements of our lives are important to God; they are God's troubles and joys too.

The late Cardinal Joseph Bernardin told a story of an old man he met on the grounds of a rest home. The man was sitting by a tree, silently meditating with a prayer book, when the cardinal came along. They chatted for a moment, and Bernardin said to him, "I imagine God loves you very much." The old man smiled, his eyes glistened, and he said, "Yes, God's very fond of me."

Think of the impact this would have on our life if we were actually, daily, aware of it.

Hardening of the Attitudes

WE ARE BORN WITH ARTERIES and attitudes that permit the healthy flow of life. Hardening of the arteries chokes the life out of our heart. Hardening of the attitudes chokes the life out of our life.

Characteristic attitudes of the young usually include idealism and optimism. Unfortunately that gradually changes. One day my senior high school students had a beneficial discussion that concerned their curiosity about why so many adults—who previously sat filled with enthusiasm and optimism in the same classroom—now, years later, seem cynical, angry, grumpy, and negative. "What happened to them that caused them to change?" the students asked. And then, closer to home, they wondered aloud, "How can we keep from turning into adults like that?"

What makes the young more idealistic and optimistic than adults? Youth have not lived as long or suffered as much. They haven't been disappointed as many times, carried as much responsibility, or felt the weight of their own mortality. Positive attitudes are easy to nurture when life is fresh and green, looking eternal. Spring has more hope than autumn. The challenge is to possess optimism in autumn and winter. The optimism of an adult is worth twice that of a young person. It has been purchased at a much higher price, with much greater discipline.

The challenges to positive attitudes increase with the events of time. Disappointments dump on us. All sorts of obstacles fall across our path. Not only do they make the traveling harder, but they attack our attitudes. "You're never going to make it," say our fears. "Life's too difficult, and you're less

43

fortunate than most people; you're weird, others are against you, and you just don't have it," our fears whisper. When we keep these notions around for a while, they become our pet thoughts, and our attitude begins to change.

Attitude is our ongoing state of mind and feeling. It's our personal climate. Attitude is gradually formed or gradually altered. We change it by what we make of the events of life and the thoughts we keep in our mind. William James, psychologist and philosopher, proclaimed, "The greatest discovery of my generation is that human beings can alter their lives by altering their attitudes of mind." Sage advice concerning the need to govern our thoughts and attitude has been offered us throughout the ages. Buddha said, "All we are is a result of what we have thought." *Practical Jung* advises those who think that an outer change—of spouse, location, or job—is more important than an inner change of thought: "Where you are is not so important as where you are when you are where your are." Expressed colloquially, "You can't change a turkey by changing his barnyard." Our thoughts influence our attitude, and our attitude influences the tenor of our life, wherever we may be.

If we stop and honestly analyze the thoughts we choose to keep in our mind, what do we discover? We might be shocked to find that most of our thoughts are angry thoughts, thoughts of being victimized, of remembering hurts and chewing over and over again what people have done to us. No wonder our general climate becomes one of anger and resentment, of being slighted. A man once told me that he analyzed his thoughts and found 75 percent of them to be about making, getting, and keeping money. No wonder his attitudinal climate didn't include much room for sensitivity, love, empathy, or appreciation for what he already has.

Many of us obtain prescriptions for cholesterol-reducing drugs. Saturated fats and cholesterol can form plaque, which in turn can clog arteries and slow down the flow of blood to the heart. We aren't learning as well how to discipline and reduce unhealthy thoughts, which form plaquelike attitudes that slow down the flow of vitality that courses through our lives.

A happy person is not a person in a certain set of circumstances but a person with a certain set of attitudes.

Our Body— Friend or Foe?

OUR BODY IS OUR DEAR friend when we're young. We feel invulnerable. Our body seems always available to serve and to gratify us. Firm and supple muscles let us run up flights of stairs, do cartwheels, engage in robust athletic activities, and dance until two in the morning. We know we can draw upon our body for endless expressions of strength and vitality. It seems always able to replenish itself no matter how we treat it. All-night studying (or partying) in college, strained muscles, a cold or the flu—all those afflictions seem so temporary. We shrug them off like a bothersome fly. We rebound quickly. We can always count on our body, our friend.

What a blow when we begin to perceive a slow transformation occurring. Perhaps it is signaled by tired legs and puffing lungs when we climb stairs, pulled hamstrings, crow's feet by our eyes, a receding hairline, or aches that don't go away so quickly. So we exercise more, oftentimes doubling our efforts. That's all it takes, we think, to keep our body as our friend.

But the unavoidable transformation continues. We soon recognize that eventual change is beyond our will, and we resent it. Notice the low-level anger we have when little injuries occur. It's not the pain, it's the inconvenience, we say. If we were completely truthful, we would admit that the unconscious recognition of our mortality hurts more than the pain. A common post-operative feeling is some degree of depression. Our body, which was once our dear friend and the servant of our ego, now seems to be our stubborn opponent.

A new attitude arises—our body becomes our enemy. Our dreams persist, but the body refuses to respond as once it did. We still wish to soar, but our body calls us back to earth.

If our goals are merely to experience eternal youth and the preservation of our physicality, then our body is indeed our betrayer. Our increasing limitations embarrass and humble us. All the joking about going downhill seems true.

But if our life is composed of more than the physical component; if the purpose of life is ultimately the development of the inner person; if spiritual qualities like love count more than lust, humility more than egotism, and wisdom more than strength, then perhaps our body is more of a friend than we realize. For it is the body, more than any other physical thing, that teaches us about the temporary nature of the world. Every day our body talks to us. It forces us to hear the message, down to the core of our being, that strength of character counts more than muscle strength. Our body and psyche work in tandem to get the point across.

Our changing body gradually erodes our pretenses and pride, revealing what we are really made of, and that what we are made of can be even more beautiful than we first thought. The body levels the playing field so that we may all be measured by the same standards of inner worth, and bids us discover both our true self and the God from whom we came and to whom we go. We are part of a mystery larger than the confines of our body and part of a magnificence greater than we can imagine.

Beethoven and Abortion

THOUGH I'M A CLASSICAL music illiterate, I find the classics conducive to reflection, reading, and tranquillity. Some studies suggest that students who study while listening to Mozart remember and perform better. True or not, millions of us are lifted by the brilliant musical talents of composers like Mozart, Tchaikovsky, Grieg, or Beethoven, whose contributions are ageless.

When we comprehend the musical genius of such people, it is as if we have opened a door and met a giant on the other side. If we compare our talent to theirs, it is as though we stand at their feet, and they rise high above us. It has taken all the centuries so far to produce the handful of exquisite musicians we enjoy today.

Beethoven's musical brilliance led me elsewhere several weeks ago when I purchased a Telarc disc of some Beethoven compositions. The promo across the front read: "Never have more inspired compositions poured from the heart and hand of a single human being. Only one composer has had such an impact on the world of music: Ludwig van Beethoven. Out of his anguish and despair unfolds music of incredible beauty and emotion." That statement is in part Telarc's hype, but it is in great part true. It is valid, based on the evidence, to surmise that centuries from now Beethoven will still intrigue the ears and hearts of countless listeners.

Not long after that, I read something else—an imagined conversation between two doctors. Though the conversation itself is concocted, the facts within it are accurate. The two doctors are discussing an actual medical situation. The first doctor speaks of a

47

mother who is tuberculous and whose husband is alcoholic and syphilitic. The first child they bore is epileptic, the second died, the third cannot speak or hear, the fourth is tuberculous. And of all things, now the mother is pregnant again. "What should she do?" asks the first doctor. Without hesitation the second doctor responds, "I would abort it! Urge her to abort it!" The first doctor replies, "You would have killed Beethoven."

Abortion causes great conflict in our society. We are very divided as we struggle with its morality. Some say resolving abortion will be analogous to the long struggle it took to resolve slavery in the nineteenth century. One thing we do know is that complex issues require our best efforts and honesty. They require philosophical, ethical, and theological examination by competent people of goodwill. Unfortunately our custom today is to draw up sides and shout at one another. The depth of our insight usually runs as deep as the thickness of a poster or bumper sticker.

The story of Beethoven may help us take pause and recommit ourself to honest searching. Since the Roe vs. Wade decision in 1973, over one million abortions a year have been performed. This means that over twenty-seven million people who might have been among us are not here. Among those millions of people was there another Beethoven? Would some of those people have been uniquely talented in research, medicine, literature, science, political life, or music? Would one of them have found a cure for cancer or heart disease? What impact might some of them have had on the world? Are we poorer without their contributions, or might one among them have been another Hitler? Only God knows. How are we to decide? *Are* we to decide?

I write to make us think, for thinking and loving are our highest powers. The resolution of problems in our homes or in our society will eventually come from the thinking and loving of people like you and me. The story of Beethoven should nudge us to thoughtfully and lovingly resolve our problems, for much is at stake. It also reminds us of the effect that one person can have on the world even though he or she may come from less than perfect origins. Each of us is worth far more than we'll ever realize.

Entering Professional Counseling

HUMAN BEINGS ARE OFTEN faced with frightening challenges: fighting in a war, skydiving, speaking to a stadium full of people. These are, perhaps, obvious examples. But add beginning sessions with a competent psychologist or psychiatrist. Surprised? Well, I agree with M. Scott Peck, MD, when he says: "Entering psychotherapy is an act of the greatest courage. The primary reason people do not undergo psychotherapy is not that they lack the money but that they lack the courage."

We give ourself many reasons not to begin counseling. Some claim it costs too much. Religious-minded people fear that psychological counselors don't believe in God and will try to talk them out of their faith. Others resist entering therapy because they are concerned that other people will think they are crazy. Some fear that others who are not in therapy will consider themselves superior to those who choose therapy. Dr. Peck, with a lifetime of experience with people in therapy, has this to say about people who enter therapy:

> It is because they possess this courage, on the other hand, that many psychoanalytic patients, even at the outset of therapy and contrary to their stereotypical image, are people who are basically much stronger and healthier than average.

Why, then, do we resist entering psychotherapy? We fear ourself. We have feelings and unhealthy parts of us that we would rather not face. We spend the first part of our life building defenses against these parts of us. In the second part of our life, around age thirty-five and after, those hidden parts begin

49

to rumble around and produce anxiety. The purpose of this anxiety is to prod us to take a look at what we have hidden and why. Delving inside ourself, alone or guided by a competent professional, is like going on a pilgrimage toward wholeness and health. At its end we find two important persons—ourself and God.

Even at the onset of therapy, we resist entering it completely. We say we want to change our life for the better. More often than not, what we really want is to stay the same and get the therapist to make us feel better. Psychotherapist Sheldon B. Kopp says of a beginning client, "He prefers the security of known misery to the misery of unfamiliar insecurity." Growth always means going into the unknown, and the unknown parts of us are frightening.

As with any professionals, some therapists are excellent, some are mediocre, and some are inadequate. Competent professionals are worth their weight in gold. The best way to find a competent therapist is to seek a referral from another trusted professional, such as a physician. Too many clergy are still threatened by the field of psychology, so they may not be the best references.

Some people mistakenly believe that the therapist provides a cure. Robert C. Murphy more accurately states: "The therapist is an observer and a catalyst. He has no power to 'cure' the patient, for cure is entirely out of his hands. He can add nothing to the patient's inherent capacity to get well. . . . The patient is already fully equipped for getting well." Though some people need medication to help them on their journey, most need only the insightful skill of their therapist and their own openness. An excellent psychologist or psychiatrist can be compared to the Statue of Liberty, which stands holding a lighted torch. In that light we must find our own way.

Therapists offer us emotional acceptance, insight, and support. They listen with the same human vulnerability we all possess. This sincere listening facilitates the telling of the patient's own story. And in telling the story of our life, and understanding it, we can be set free.

The growth of so many good people has been temporarily slowed or fixed at a certain stage. This results in increasing stress, anxiety, and a sense of being empty, depressed, or separated from oneself. A wonderful thing happens when a person picks up from where he or she is stuck and continues to develop spiritually and psychologically. Though initially frightening, going down this road less traveled, as Robert Frost says, makes all the difference.

In the Teeth of Doubt

WHAT ARE WE TO DO about our doubts? Act like they're not there, or feel guilty when they appear? Does that mean our faith is not strong enough? Shouldn't we have everything all figured out?

We all have doubts. Doubts about life, self, God, relationships, you name it. This is because we are rational, and our intellects are made for truth—to seek it, find it, know it, and grasp it. As we become more mature, the doubts that trouble us the most are doubts about God and spiritual matters. This is an area where reason can take us only so far; then we are called to leap into what is scientifically unprovable. As we weigh making the leap, doubt creeps in. How understandable! A mind and heart are too precious to commit recklessly, casually.

The problem is that in the crucial decisions of life, we want to know the whole truth right away, not gradually. Our ego's top priority is security. We want to be sure, to know we're right, to know whether where we leap has a firm bottom upon which to land. Doubt is unwelcome. At times we are frightened, overwhelmed, or paralyzed by it. The German word for doubt is *zweifeln,* "twoness," because when we experience doubt, we feel we are divided in two, straddling two paths that go in different directions. Which one should we choose?

Though doubt is normal, some can't stand it because they can't bear to think that they may be wrong or that they don't have all the answers. Spiritual life deals with the existence of God, the afterlife, moral decision making, and so on. In concerns of such immense significance, some are troubled to find ambiguity and grayness standing in the way

51

of absolute certitude. Threatened by doubts, some people repress or deny them. Others need to see themselves as sure and right, so they build their own orthodoxy around the cornerstone of their doubts.

But doubt need not be negative and threatening. Doubt is a positive reality. God is a vast and wonderful mystery, beyond the grasp of our poor minds. Theologian Bernard Häring, in his book *The Virtues of an Authentic Life,* even has a chapter entitled "Cultivating the Virtue of Healthy Doubt." Author and minister Frederick Buechner has a marvelous way to express the positive side of doubts: "Doubts are the ants in the pants of faith. They keep it awake and moving." Certainty is the enemy of growth toward fuller truth. If we have God figured out, God must not be much to figure. Any of us who expect to grow and go deeper into the mystery of God must be willing, from time to time, to doubt, then search, discuss, struggle, and break old categories. The most important thing is to accompany doubts with healthy attempts to resolve them. Bede Jarrett expresses well our situation, "The truth may be one, final, determined, but my apprehension of it can never be anything of the kind; it is changing continuously."

Spiritual doubts intensify during adolescence. They prod us to move forward and shift from a secondhand faith (the beliefs given to us by our parents) to a firsthand faith (the beliefs we choose for ourself). Unfortunately some parents get anxious when their teens express doubt about long-held family beliefs. Some even take it as personal rejection. In reality such doubt is something to celebrate, as when a baby tooth falls out to make room for the grown-up version. It is a sign of maturation.

Periods of intensified doubt continue throughout adult life and are often precipitated by life events like marriage, a death in the family, the experience of suffering, or the witnessing of cruelty and evil in the world. Each time, if we respond to them well, doubts can lead us to consider and solidify our own firsthand faith. Just as we cannot go through life with baby teeth, we cannot resolve the doubts of adulthood with the pieties of childhood. Doubts must be met by reflection on the scriptures of one's religion; discussions with competent people; and periods of prayer, study, and silence. The God with whom we deal is a loving and understanding God who loves us far more than our doubts can separate us.

Apathy, Sympathy, Empathy

HOW OFTEN DO YOU FEEL *really* understood? From whom do you receive that understanding—your spouse? a parent? a friend? We long to experience resonance with another human being. Our longing begins the day we're born, and it ends the day we die.

In psychological terminology that is part of a dynamic called mirroring, which happens when one person receives, registers, and reflects back to another some of the other's inner hidden self. The more we are understood by another, the more treasured is the occurrence and the more appreciated is the person. In spiritual terminology such an acceptance can even be spoken of as an act of love or compassion.

Genuine understanding is highly beneficial, so it is helpful to recognize what occurs when we receive it, and whether we give this exquisite gift to others. *Apathy, sympathy,* and *empathy* are three words that express three very different ways of considering human understanding. Let's look at all three.

Apathy is a lack of connection. An apathetic person does not connect with what we really are feeling. We have no resonance. If we are apathetic in our dealings with others, we hear them speaking, but we fail to listen. Our approach is totally rational, detached, and objective. We focus accurately on the ideas and facts given us, we can give adequate advice if it is sought, but distance remains. A courtroom judge may find this helpful in administering impartial justice, but among spouses or friends it is exasperating. Apathy is an obstacle to understanding. Children who experience ongoing apathy from their parents suffer because their parents are distant. On

53

the other hand, when we feel understood by others, especially on a regular basis, we say we are close to them.

Sympathy goes beyond the understanding of factual information and includes feeling. A resonance in feelings exists between persons. The personal situation of one person induces a reciprocal set of feelings in another. One person feels "with" the other and experiences the same sentiments of joy, sorrow, sadness. Sympathetic relationships lack objectivity, encourage over-identification, and often result in unhealthy rescue attempts. Our sympathy may be appreciated by another, but it often renders us unable to advise them well. That's why, for example, a family member who is a physician or a psychologist usually refers family members to someone else for medical care or counseling.

Empathy, on the other hand, is a more intellectual identification with, or a vicarious experiencing of, the feelings, thoughts, or attitudes of another. We listen well and respond to another individual's feelings in a compassionate way, but without sharing them. We don't panic if that person panics, we don't grieve as that person grieves, yet we are tuned in to that person's experience. Empathy is an essential prerequisite for good parents, a "best friend" spouse, a genuine friend, or a competent counselor. We must be able to empathetically focus on the feelings of other people if we hope for some true connection with them. People in caring professions must be capable of empathetic listening to be truly effective.

In our personal interactions with others, we can experience a variety of responses. Some people seem to be listening to us, but we soon realize that they have missed our feelings or don't want to know them. They are listening only to facts, or perhaps they are thinking about their agenda and what they are going to say to us next. They are apathetic listeners. The people who enrich our existence are those who listen accurately to what we say *and* what we don't say. This doesn't mean they always approve, but they embody a nonjudgmental attitude that accepts us as we are. We feel comfortable with them. We can only explain that comfort by saying, "They understand us."

God and the *Quid Pro Quo*

WHERE HAS GRATITUDE GONE? Our primary focus is on our rights. We believe we are owed everything. We perceive ourself to be self-made, self-sufficient, and deserving. We feel we have paid our way, or that fate has randomly favored us, or that we are special people who are owed more in life than others. With these attitudes, who needs to be grateful?

We lose gratitude when we lose the sense of gift. We commonly understand the concept of gift as something expected or owed, not freely and spontaneously given. Birthdays, anniversaries, Mother's Day, Father's Day, Valentine's Day, and all the other days for everyone from grandparents to secretaries to bosses are days promoted by profit-making industries to entice us to buy and give things. In the current climate, we are likely to give because we feel that we must or to avoid guilt or to curry favor or so that we meet another's expectations.

The result? A real gift is rarely given. The best gifts are spontaneous, unexpected, and have no strings attached. Real gifts arise from the heart rather than the calendar. They are not part of games like, "I give you this, now you be and do as I say." They are not the buying of affection, friendship, political consideration, or attention. They are not once-a-year cancellations of yearlong insensitivity. Real gifts are as rare today as real love.

God is the ultimate gift-giver, giving us life, uniqueness, and all the good things that ever happen to us. If God did not sustain us in existence each moment, we would disappear. If God did not help us, we would fail.

Speaking in a spiritual way, we use the word *grace* for all the different gifts God gives us. A succinct definition of the theological meaning of *grace* is that it is "the freely given, unmerited favors and love of God." The word *grace* comes from the Latin word *gratis,* meaning favor or kindness. Grace is unearned. God's favors are free. They are *gratis.* And where hard times and sin abound, grace abounds all the more.

Perhaps you have heard the story of a young businessman from the East, making his first trip to the South. When he drove into South Carolina the first morning, he was really hungry. He stopped at a roadside diner. He ordered eggs, sausage, and toast. When the meal came, he was surprised to see a white blob of something on his plate. "What's this?" he asked the waitress. "Them's grits, suh," she answered in her strong southern accent. "But I didn't order them," he said. "You don't order grits," she replied, "it just comes." Same for God's grace—it just comes. Because God loves us exceedingly, God's grace is always around nudging, helping, supporting, healing.

It is sad to watch people trying to do business with God, trying to buy God. Novenas, a good work done here or there, a donation of money, are often attempts to barter with God. "I'll give you this, God, and you give me that," we think. Political action committee representatives have nothing on us. Our intentions are good, but we use our imperfect human ways of dealing with others in our dealings with God. But God cannot be bought. All is grace. All is gift. God is constantly showering good things on us simply out of love for us, but in our spiritual naiveté, we shelter ourself with an invisible umbrella that "protects" us from grace.

As we grow spiritually, we begin to see through different eyes. We close the umbrella of naiveté that shielded us from the gifts falling all over us. We begin to see reality differently. Not that we see things that aren't there; rather we begin to see things that have always been there but had gone unrecognized. The presence of so many gifts and the love that they imply stuns us. We feel so fortunate. And that gives birth to the only appropriate word: *thanks.*

Grief: Love's Dark Companion

IN *CHILDREN'S LETTERS TO GOD,* a little girl named Jane writes, "Dear God, Instead of letting people die and having to make new ones, why don't you just keep the ones you got now?"

Cute! Jane is apparently trying to save God some work, but she is also motivated by her own self-interest. She is beginning to realize that she will feel grief when someone she loves dies.

No other experience in our travels is more recurrent than loss. Life begins with loss when we are ejected from the protective womb, disconnected from the heartbeat that comforted us with a security we expected to last forever. Then off we go, impelled forward on a journey that ends with the loss of life itself. Along the way are multiple findings and losings. Loss is central to the human condition and is a constant insult to our desire to be immortal, to be as God, to have ownership of the tree of life.

Also constant is the concomitant to loss —grief. As Rainer Maria Rilke says, "So we live, forever saying farewell." Farewell to stages of life, people, places, moments owned then lost. We might expect to be accomplished in dealing with loss and grief, but we're not.

If we choose to love, we must have the courage to grieve. To live is to know that that is true. Each heart has its times to grieve. Each heart has its own sacred dramas. Each of us is changed in different ways by our experience of love and grief.

Is grief useless? Is loss only a waste? That depends on the heart that is hurt. At one end of the spectrum are hearts that become more compassionate as the result of loss. The losses we experience can open us to others. We develop a sympathetic camaraderie that enables us to be softly in touch with the hearts of others. We become wounded healers.

At the other end of the spectrum are frightened souls who have not mourned losses and whose wounds remain raw and untended. We withdraw from pain, grief, and loss because the gaping hole seems too devouring. We feel we will lose ourself in the awesome ache of emptiness and never find ourself again. From then on we flee both grief and love, fearing love will be the beginning of the end.

Grieving is good for us. Its purpose is to heal. Mourning can be redemptive, creative; it has all the power of love and more. Some of our finest breakthroughs in humanness are achieved in times of grief. Grief forges an inner expansiveness and kinship with God and humankind. Only those who carry the illusion of omnipotence expect never to grieve. The day after the assassination of President John F. Kennedy, one of his relatives, Kenny O'Donnell, said on the radio, "What's the use of being Irish if you don't know that sooner or later the world will break your heart?"

James Hollis expresses superbly what can happen to us at times of grief and loss: "Somewhere, in the collision between heart, which longs for permanency and connection, and brain, which acknowledges separation and loss, there is a place for us to find our personal psychology," and I would hasten to add, our personal faith, as well. In the awful collision of heart and mind, we have only two alternatives: We can fashion meaning and trust, or we can sink into the strangling depths of cynical despair.

Loss and grief offer us the opportunity to fully appreciate someone of value who has been part of our life. Where we experience no loss, we experience no value. Loss initiates what mystics call the *via negativa*—"the negative way"—the dark womb from which a birth can eventually happen. In a life of changes and choices, it can be our grand consolation to realize that we were freely given a place in the heart of another. Holding to this exquisite privilege, and letting go of control, is the double work of loss and grief.

A *Joie de Vivre* That Lasts Forever

LIFE AND DEATH. Too often we think of them as *yes* and *no*. How inadequate! Death certainly could be considered as one harsh *no*, but life is a long *yes* with many degrees. Life is like the full spectrum of light, consisting of many beautiful colors and all their shades. There are differing shades of being alive.

If life could be placed on a dimmer switch, like the ones we sometimes use for electric lights, we could see the degrees of life by turning the knob. Turned low, light can be so dim it is almost imperceptible. As we turn up the dimmer, the light becomes brighter and brighter until it becomes so intense that we must look away.

Life is like that. There is a dim, depressed, empty way of being alive that prompts one to moan in cynical misery, "You call this living?" From this low point on its spectrum, life has unlimited potential for increasing in meaning and satisfying intensity. Perhaps we all have experienced sporadic occasions when life was so fulfilling and our joy so great that it seemed uncontainable, times when life splashed over the brim of our heart, and we felt like laughing and shouting in affirmation, "Now *this* is living!"

I've always liked the French expression, *joie de vivre*. Sometimes we reach out for an expression in another language because our feelings go beyond our everyday words. *Joie de vivre* packs into three mysterious words the exquisite feeling of the hearty delight of being alive.

Joie de vivre, the "joy of life," is a hint of heaven. It is life with the dimmer switch turned all the way up. It is enthusiasm spread to every corner of our being.

Easter celebrates life. We Christians believe that God raised up the dead Jesus Christ on the first Easter Day. But his Resurrection means much more than the resuscitation of a dead corpse. It means a transformation of this life, offered to one and all. His rising is like the first eruption of a volcano, which shows that in the interior of the world, God's life is always churning. Eventually it will prevail and bring everything to fullness of life. Easter is the ultimate feast on the Christian calendar, greater than Christmas. Christ's rising demonstrates and promises an eternal *joie de vivre* that is already under way.

Among the secular symbols of this feast are soft things like baby chicks, blossoms, and bunnies—fragile, delicate, fluffy things. Yet real life is anything but delicate, especially in springtime, Eastertime, when life's forward force calls blades of grass to grow through cracks in concrete and chicks to break through hard shells. The call to a full and intense life is such an imperative, for God has only *full* life in mind for us. We back off at our own risk.

We Live by Mending

LENT IS NO ONE'S favorite time. For the Christian churches that celebrate it, Lent is a six-week period of personal repentance and spiritual growth. It is a time of self-discipline, acknowledgment of personal sinfulness, and genuine attempts to improve one's spiritual life. It is as welcome as football training camp to an out-of-shape rookie, boot camp to a new Marine, or intense dance classes for a fledgling ballerina. By nature we dislike self-discipline. We prefer self-gratification. Sacrifice for anything but self-serving goals seems useless and masochistic.

Lent exists because we are dancing here for just a short while. The season begins with foreheads smudged with ashes that carry the solemn reminder that "into dust you shall return." This solid dose of reality challenges us to acknowledge our limits and appreciate life all the more. Knowing we will someday die enables us to guide our life accordingly. Most religions believe—in one way or another—that life goes on for us after we die to this world. While we're here, we are supposed to grow as people—to become more altruistic, compassionate, whole, holy, loving. We are to know and serve the God who made us, and love the people God has made.

Our ego gets in the way, though, and makes that a difficult task. If asked at an early age why we are here, we would all say, "Me!" If asked whether there was a Supreme Being, we would all say, "Yes, me!" If asked whether others count, we would say, "If they please me!" The goal of our spiritual life is to unlearn these illusions and to learn to love. A character in Eugene O'Neill's play *The Great God Brown,* says: "Man is born broken. He lives by mending. The grace of God is glue."

We are imperfect. We need to grow into our potential, and in order to accomplish this growth, we need God.

Lent is a time of concentrated mending, a time to make a quantum step forward and turn away from our predominant weakness or sin, and a time to let God accomplish some healing within us. How we do that is different for each of us, but it does require perceptive insight. For example, a friend might announce that he or she is going on a diet during Lent. The diet, however, seems to be an attempt to try and kill two birds with one stone. And the bigger bird often has nothing to do with spiritual growth, but with looking better in next summer's swimsuit. That's fine, but Lenten spiritual growth requires a deeper awareness of our inner sins and weaknesses. With clearer insight such a dieter might realize that her or his weakness is too much concern about physical attractiveness, and not enough about the needs of others. That person might go ahead and diet for the summer swimsuit, but a better spiritual choice might be to look beyond physical form by visiting people in rest homes during Lent, and to look past the wrinkled faces and shaking hands to discover interior beauty.

Other possibilities for Lent? For a couple whose relationship and love for each other is deteriorating due to busyness, a solution might be to get a baby-sitter and go out to dinner twice a week. For those who sense that their lives are meaningless and empty, seeking silent times for reading, prayer, or introspection may help. For those to whom God is a stranger, attending church every week may help. For those who recognize that they have been excessively materialistic, giving anonymous financial help to others in legitimate need may help. The ways to spend a good Lent, and mend a broken life, are as unique as each individual soul.

The creation of the world is ongoing. Our personal creation is ongoing. God wants, with our cooperation, to continue making something beautiful of our lives. At the end of each biblical day of creation, God beamed about what he had made and said, "That's good!" At the end of the last day, when he created humans, God intensified his exclamation. He looked at us and said, "That's *very* good!" As we mend, with God's grace as our glue, God continues to say, "That's *very* good!"

Moral Relativism

WE HEAR A LOT TODAY about how Johnny can't read, can't write, and can't find France on the map. It is also true that Johnny and Suzy have difficulty distinguishing right from wrong. Young people seem to know little about moral tradition and its deep-seated logic.

Shirley Jackson's short story "The Lottery" is a tale of a small farming community that seems normal in every way. As the plot progresses, however, the reader learns a secret about this community. Each year its residents hold a lottery in which the loser is stoned to death. "The Lottery" is supposed to warn about the dangers of mindless conformity. But in high school and college class discussions about the story, more and more students are backing down from taking a definite stand against human sacrifice. "Who am I to condemn them?" is an oft repeated observation. "If that's the way they want to run their town and their lives, that's up to them. Those who don't like it can move away."

Moral life issues today are usually a mental stew made up of a jumble of facts, opinions, and little real thinking. Students learn that the early Aztecs offered annual human sacrifices—they offered a young virgin to their gods. Students today also learn of the benefits of multicultural understanding—that they should welcome diversity rather than fear it. Students live in an age in which society is divided by moral issues like abortion, euthanasia, the death penalty, suicide, marital fidelity, and many others, of which the answers seem to be guided by whatever works best for the individual rather than by any moral principles. During the turmoil over the Clinton infidelities, students listened as many adults proclaimed, "As long as he's running the country well, it doesn't matter what he does personally or if he lied under oath."

Although it is true that we must debate many controversial issues, we must not forget the core of noncontroversial ethical issues that were settled a long time ago.

We are overdosing on nonjudgmentalism. Many adults perceive themselves as having been raised too rigidly, suffocated by overly strict discipline or religious judgments of well-meaning parents, clergy, and teachers. Wanting to free themselves of such rigidity, they now run to the other extreme and eschew *any* judgments. The result? We are drowning in a sea of moral relativism. Everything is up for grabs.

Despite the beliefs passed down through the ages, postmodern theory denies the existence of a core of objective moral truths. Once these norms are forgotten, or are reduced to being seen merely as clashing perspectives or outdated customs, moral laziness sets in. The governing moral principles become: "If it feels good, do it"; "If you want to, why not?"; "This is a free country, and I have my rights!"; "Nobody can tell me what to do."

When God is left out of the picture and thinking is at a minimum, moral laws are arbitrary.

We need to think, study, understand. The core issues of morality are not arbitrary. They are based on who and what humans are, on our nature and what is of value to it. Our nature stays the same, so the basic moral core stays the same. Some choices that were wrong in the second century are still wrong in the twenty-first century, and will be wrong in the twenty-fifth century. It will always be wrong for me to steal your property, your money, your good reputation, or your life because of my cruelty or selfish interests. Those things, and others, will always be wrong; some values will always be right. Neither our individual lives, nor the communal life of a society, can survive for long on lies, deceit, and injustice.

God did not arbitrarily think up these values in order to take the fun out of life. These values flow from who we are and how we must behave if we are to become whole, integrated persons who believe and trust one another, make contracts, and live an ordered, happy life. All morality—sexual, relational, and corporate—comes from the dictates of our nature, from the way we've been made by God. Freedom means choosing what we ought. License means choosing only what we want. Johnny and Suzy and many others in their community need to learn the difference.

Near-Life Experiences

HAVE YOU EVER READ of someone who had a near-death experience? The trauma of a life-threatening heart attack or car accident seems to thrust some people into a different mode of existence. They perceive themselves as outside their body, observing from above. They watch medical personnel administering to their body. Instead of feeling pain or fear, they experience an exquisite inner peace. They report seeing a light at the end of a tunnel, smiling figures of loved relatives, or God. After their body is resuscitated, they resume their life, but with one big difference: they no longer fear death as they did before.

Given the occurrence of near-death experiences, might there be near-*life* experiences as well? Don't soul-grabbing events remind us how wonderful life can be? Isn't it possible to sporadically get lost, not in a life-threatening trauma or drug-induced high, but in positively rich human situations that lift us above the ordinary?

Such occasions begin to come unexpectedly when we are young. We get lifted above the everyday by the gift of a new toy, the thrill of an intense athletic game, the excitement of a first kiss, or an applause for a noteworthy accomplishment. Throughout life they continue: We become so mesmerized by the ocean and tumbling surf that we become oblivious to time and place, a young father is stunned and awe-stricken as he experiences his first child being born, a mother cries tears of joy and sees her daughter in a whole new way as the daughter walks up the aisle on her wedding day.

Instead of looking beyond the gateway of death, near-life experiences draw us deeply into the here and now, beyond the doorway of routine and distraction. They draw us into a more expansive sense of reality, reminding us of what life is and can be.

Near-life experiences can happen at any time. The important thing is that they happen. We need to be coaxed to enter life. Cynicism, fear, and routine can freeze us until we are numb. We need to be reminded that life is a deep mystery that often takes place while we pass by on our way to less important things. Life is to be fathomed and lived intensely, not considered a series of tragedies to be endured until we sleep. Near-death experiences help us not to fear death. Near-life experiences help us not to fear life.

At first that sounds strange, doesn't it? To suggest that it is possible to fear life? We tell ourself we want life, enjoy life, crave life. Oh, but we can fool ourself! Don't we too often pull back from life to maintain our security, meet cultural expectations, or sidestep the risks involved in commitment and responsibility? Paradoxically we dread intensely fulfilling experiences because we know we'll have to leave them, or because they may lead us to expect more of ourself in the future. We know that to *really* enter into the experience of life, we will have to face our fears. We will feel our joys more intensely, but we will feel our sufferings as well.

We cannot live intensely and at the same time accept only the good feelings while avoiding the bad. So we choose to compromise. To keep from meeting our fearful feelings, we are willing to avoid meeting our positive ones as well. We agree to live in the Land of In-between.

If we ever decide to leave the dull Land of In-between, we must be willing to become more fully human. We must take our own life in hand and face all that comes rather than run. We must battle our fearful demons, face up to hard choices, and make them. At times we will feel vulnerable and overwhelmed, as though we're losing the battle. Yet even the fear of losing must be faced, or the life experience of triumph will not be found. We must face our doubts about God if we are to meet God. We must know our vulnerable self if we are to ever welcome home a stronger self.

What No Eye Has Seen

"WHAT NO EYE HAS SEEN and no ear has heard, what the mind of man cannot visualize; all that God has prepared for those who love him" (1 Corinthians 2:9, NJB).

Think of what that means! In this world our imagination exceeds reality, but when we think of the life to come, reality exceeds our imagination. Let's look at the first part of this statement. With our fertile imagination, we are able to imagine things in this world that do not exist in reality. By way of example, try this simple exercise. Read the following paragraph and see how vividly you can imagine the things described.

Envision a lake that is two miles long and one mile wide. The lake is completely filled with hot chocolate. Several huge Air Force cargo planes fly over the horizon. One after the other, they dump tons of vanilla ice cream into the middle of the lake until it is stacked seventy-five feet high. For the final touch, a large helicopter flutters in and lowers a large maraschino cherry onto the very top of the vanilla ice cream heap.

You can imagine that scene. You can see it, even though it doesn't exist. Or if I speak of a planet of solid gold, whirling in space, glistening in the bright sunlight, you can imagine it, even though it doesn't exist in reality. Imagination can take us beyond the limits of the natural order.

The quotation from First Corinthians, however, tells us that the opposite situation occurs when we try to think of the life to come, the life that "God has prepared" for us. The reality of the supernatural order *exceeds* our capability to imagine it. We cannot imagine, even with the most creative effort of our imagination, what our experience will be with God.

Even with our powerful imagination, we think too small when it comes to God. Should that surprise us? No, but it does. We have the tendency to measure God in terms of the world. In fact, much of the time we see ourself as better than God—more understanding, more alive, more aware of how best to handle every situation. Our prayers frequently inform God of what should be done rather than seek enlightenment or express trust.

To think that we are loved so prodigally by a God who has unimaginable gifts prepared for us is extremely encouraging, but at the same time mystifying. The concept often seems too utterly hopeful and extravagant, so we belittle it. We brush it off as childish gullibility, or consider it to be pie-in-the-sky quackery, or seek an ironic comfort zone in a more cut-and-dried, fire-and-brimstone approach to God. These choices save us from the difficulty of dealing with someone who feels so passionately about us.

Some doubt the existence of God because they conceive of God as too dispassionate, distant, and permissive of suffering. What a twist, then, when others doubt because the God of lavish loving and giving is inconceivable to them. They think such promises are only some grand, projected, human wish, a remnant from the days of fairy tales.

Our technological skills permit us to create complex computers, amazing spaceships, and worldwide communication links, but we intellectually whittle God down to a manageable, imaginable size. The only problem is, what we fashion isn't the real One. What it comes down to is well expressed by the mystic Meister Eckhart: "The idea of God can become the final obstacle to God."

Projection

WHEN WE GO to the movies, we see not only a film but a demonstration of the psychological dynamic called projection. The pictures on the screen are only projections, images placed on the screen from somewhere else. The actual images are to be found on the film in the projector at the back of the room.

This is what we do any time we project. We project or transfer a characteristic of ourself onto others. This very popular defense mechanism works by placing aspects of ourself in somebody else, where we can safely comment on them. A parent who is a perfectionist is rarely pleased with the efforts of his or her children. Projection permits us to handle our own problems in a very roundabout manner, protecting ourself from truths that would upset us if we faced them directly. If we have traits that we unconsciously hate, we will usually experience that hatred when we see those traits in other people. Conceited persons who do not recognize their own proud conceit, for example, will strongly dislike others who demonstrate conceit. In such cases, even the advice we often give to children is valuable: If you point out a fault in someone else, look at your hand—three fingers are pointing back at you.

We seldom learn anything new about ourself by direct observation. Usually it is only after seeing a particular characteristic in someone else—and experiencing strong feelings about it—that we can begin to recognize it as our own. This takes a lot of honesty. So much of our interior life is beyond our conscious awareness, but it nonetheless affects us and moves us emotionally. Becoming more psychologically and spiritually healthy means that we gradually become more and more conscious of what is going on in our unconscious.

For example, occasionally we hear of a clergyman who is obsessed with sexual behavior and is angry at the licentious lives of others. Then we may be stunned by the news that this clergyman has been arrested for molesting a teenager, or that he has become a voyeur on the Internet. Analysis will likely reveal that the clergyman was unwittingly preaching against his own unconscious sexual desires. He permitted himself to see them only in others, found them frightening, but failed to realize them in himself. Had he come to realize his projections sooner, he would have had the opportunity to deal with his own desires more realistically and healthfully—and then been better able to help others.

If we want to know more about ourself, we can ask, "Who, or what behavior, disturbs me greatly?" The intensity of my answer is what is revealing. Or we can make a list of ten traits that irritate us in other people. Then from that list, we select the three or four traits that most strongly trouble us. The odds are that deep within us we have tendencies toward those irritating behaviors. When we ask ourself why such behavior upsets us so much, we learn a lot about ourself.

Such a practice is invaluable in human relationships. We can hardly have a conscious, satisfying relationship with another if we have a deeply wounded relationship with ourself. All that we do not know about ourself, all unresolved wounds experienced throughout our life, we tend to impose on others. When we recognize our projections, we enhance our satisfying relationships. We can learn a lot about ourself by unscrambling the feelings we project onto other people.

Discovering our unconscious projections is not just psychological, spiritually freeing work. Though the term was not used in his day, Jesus Christ spoke of our tendency to project when he asked, "Why do you see the speck in your neighbor's eye, but do not notice the log in your own?" (Matthew 7:3). Jesus clearly understood that self-knowledge is best developed in the light of how we deal with others.

We can work to understand our projections on our own. However, the opportunity to disentangle our projections and know ourself is found most richly in psychotherapy, solid friendships, or marriage. That is why truthful, communicative, and long-term committed relationships generally contribute more to our growth than do shorter ones. If we can be honest and humble enough, we will meet ourself in the ups and downs of our dealings with others.

The Pursuit of Happiness

DON'T WE HAVE the impression that all our work and effort is eventually supposed to make us happy? Don't we imagine that if we keep climbing the mountain of life, we'll someday reach a plateau of soft green grass called happiness? Aren't we promised happiness by the U.S. Constitution? Not really. We are promised that we can pursue it. That doesn't define it or guarantee that we will catch it. Gurus paint this picture: Happiness is like a butterfly. Try to catch the butterfly and it will escape you. But if you ignore it, it may come and sit on your shoulder. That sounds nice, but it is frustrating to wait, hoping happiness will come. It always seems to pass us by or land on someone else's shoulder.

What is happiness, anyway? Happiness comes when we are aware that we possess something good. If I think a new sports car is good, and I get one, I'm happy because I possess something good. If I think being married is good, and I marry, I feel happy. One characteristic of happiness, though, is that it fades. Something else catches our eye, and we begin to imagine how happy we will be if only we could have it. We see this in children and their toys. And adults, no matter what they have, seem to conclude that they will be happy if only they could have one more million, one more spouse, one more chance to live youth over again.

We are never as happy as we expect to be. From a religious perspective, our heart and mind have been made ultimately for God, and nothing but God can fill us completely. The happiness called heaven is beyond anything we find or experience here. Happiness is also elusive because the goal of life is not just to find happiness, but to find meaning.

71

Carl Jung writes:

I have frequently seen people become neurotic when they content themselves with inadequate or wrong answers to the questions of life. They seek position, marriage, reputation, outward success or money, and remain unhappy and neurotic even when they have attained what they were seeking. Such people are usually confined within too narrow a spiritual horizon. Their life has not sufficient content, sufficient meaning. If they are enabled to develop into more spacious personalities, the neurosis generally disappears.

We don't often start asking ourself these important questions, the questions that lead to meaning, until we arrive at midlife or after (if we do it at all). Cultural philosophy tells us that happiness will come from getting and having, from being king or queen of the hill. As we reach midlife, we begin to wonder where the happiness is. We have been pursuing happiness all along, at least according to materialistic definitions, so shouldn't we have much of it by now? When we reach this point, we are more prepared to seek meaning.

We begin to realize that meaning comes from within, not from without. We start to grapple with the mystery of life and of our own person. We become engaged in soul work, being led within, to our deepest core. This is the hardest task we will ever face. We are frightened by the thought of entering into the realm of our deepest feelings and motives. But if we don't start trying to discover meaning in our life, we become ill—mentally, physically, or emotionally. The pursuit of true happiness leads us down a road we never imagined. Our youthful dreams saw life as all sweetness and light. We find out that it requires going through darkness, work, defeat, suffering, puzzlement, and brokenheartedness. Only then comes the meaning. Then comes the sweetness and the life.

Quiet Desperation

"THE MASS OF MEN lead lives of quiet desperation," Thoreau says at the beginning of *Walden.* What a sad state of affairs. Thoreau is speaking of the desperation that results from the lack of any great hope, the lack of any great thing to live for. Quietness is the way of despair—we feel we are being silently smothered with boredom and futility. There's no way out. One woman described it like this: "It seems that even if I should scream as loud as I can, nothing will change, and after the echo of my voice fades away, everything will settle back to usual."

What brings some to this sad state? Such somber feelings can, of course, be manifestations of clinical depression. Prolonged depression is most healthfully dealt with in a psychologist's or psychiatrist's office over time. Occasionally physiological factors are present that indicate medication is also necessary.

The experience of loss—the death of someone we love, the ending of an important relationship, the loss of a job—can also cause depressive and desperate feelings. Nor are our feelings exempt from the impact of significant events and changes in our life, like suffering from an illness, going through menopause, moving, becoming a single parent, seeing our children grow up and leave home. Life contains many necessary losses and changes.

Depression can also arise if we suppress the life force within us. We move on a continuum, through successive transitions that enlarge our potential. We become our own enemy when we stifle this drive toward a fuller life, leading ourself to experience depression, feelings of incompleteness, emptiness, and the sense that something is missing.

Our inner life has been compared to a deep well. All kinds of things down at the bottom of our well comprise us and affect our life. At the bottom of our well we will find the parts and pieces, the unknown factors, that can bring understanding and lead us to find hope and meaning in our life. To swim down to the bottom of our well is an exceptionally difficult task, but it is the way out of despair; it is the way toward growth. Something in the deep well of our person will shine a light on our quiet desperation.

If we look around, we will always find people who have every reason to feel desperate, yet have plunged into their darkest times to fight it. Author John Carmody, suffering from cancer that would eventually kill him, fought not only the cancer but the moods that would try to beat him down:

> Though I have terminal cancer, I can still register a brilliant sunrise, a quick dash of wit from a friend, the great legs on the brunette in the brown tights and short skirt. Though I have to start a new round of chemotherapy in the afternoon there is time for a nice lunch, and it would be perverse not to take it, enjoy it, roll it around my tongue and let it gladden my spirit. When I have a will to discover beauty in the world, things to celebrate, I am apt to find them. When I fight my temptations to depression, I feel more like a man.

Happy, healthy times don't often make us search out meaning. But in the desperate times, we must heed the call to dive deeper, to look, and to search for identity and meaning. Quiet desperation is not meant to lead to personal defeat, but to understanding and triumph.

From Religion to Spirituality

THIS IS NOT AN ESSAY knocking religion. This is an essay about the quality of our religion and how it comes about.

Our first impressions in life do not include God. The more undeveloped we are, the more we feel that *we* are God. As infants we are the center of the universe. Our needs must be met immediately, and our parents are our servants. We don't know how to give, only to get. With some alterations, such perceptions continue into adolescence. We feel indestructible, godlike, and others stand as frustrating restrictions to our freedom. Feeling like that, who needs to acknowledge and worship some other God when we have ourself? Religion is a peripheral issue of life, like rules of etiquette and traffic laws. If we belong to an organized religion, it may be more like belonging to a club. Our heart is not in it.

When we start to take on some of the hard knocks of life, when we experience evidence of our mortality, we become more willing to admit that there might be Someone else greater than us. However, we still see this Being as one who infringes on our freedom, as a distant rule-monger to be placated and appeased in order to get what we want. Even for many adults, our motives for practicing a religion are often self-serving or rooted in fear. We pray and go to church to please God and to ward off punishment and hard times. We seek God's favor, afraid of what might happen to us if we don't—there might be hell to pay in this world or the next.

As life goes on, we inevitably experience hard times—we could call them our personal hells. (Pity the person who doesn't encounter them!) We lose our job, someone

75

we love dies, our spouse has an affair, one of our kids is on drugs, or we discover a suspicious lump in our body. God suddenly becomes more necessary. We cry out, angry, wondering why God lets these things happen to us. "What have I done to deserve these trips to 'hell'? I thought being religious would prevent such things." Some people decide never to return to church after experiencing traumas, attempting, in a way, to punish God.

After many hardships, after enough time goes by for self-reflection and honesty, we begin to see more clearly. Wisdom follows wounds. We begin to ask ourself some of the essential questions of life: Who am I? Why am I here, and where am I going? Why do I suffer? The answers that eventually come expose us to truth and to some strange paradoxes about life. With these questions we become engaged in spirituality, not just religion.

We enter into spirituality when we realize that we are not God, that the world does not revolve around us, that we are imperfect creatures loved by God despite our imperfections. Spirituality plants our feet firmly on the ground and gives us a vision of ourself as we are—good but weak and vulnerable. Spirituality empties us of pretense, pride, and illusions of omnipotence. It teaches us that there is only one God, and we are not it. Spirituality is present when our prayer becomes a cry for help: "O Lord, make haste to help me" (Psalm 70:1).

The paradoxes we learn from our developing spirituality teach us that through loss we can actually gain; through hard times we come to good times; through sufferings and deaths, we find life. We discover that much of our belief in God has been based on being rescued from troubles, but that through having troubles we actually come to believe and love more deeply. What we gain from our personal hells plays a critical role in our lives.

When our spiritual life begin in earnest, our relationship with God takes a quantum leap. The God we thought we were when we were young is gone. We see ourself as a mere human, and we see the real God as a magnificent and mysterious Being. The God with whom we thought we could barter or make a deal to ward off dangers turns out to be a God who doesn't want anything but our heart. We finally recognize the God we thought was a list of rules as the Lover of our soul. The One we thought sent the troubles is the One who helps us struggle through them. The hard times of our hells have opened our eyes to the wonders of reality.

How Many Times Does Spring Come Around?

IF WE CONSIDER the revolving earth, we know springtime comes around often—every year. If we consider the overall flow of our lives as one set of four seasons, then we might say that spring comes only once—when we are young. Youth lives in springtime and, oh, how we remember the delightful moods of springtime—bursting enthusiasm, spontaneity, feelings of freedom and romance, and life with no lid on it. Those of us who are now older recall our youth as a time when a zesty *joie de vivre* ran alongside us as warm winds tousled our hair. We envy those who are young. Why shouldn't we? If spring comes only once, who wouldn't have a tinge of envy toward those who have it now?

But *does* spring come only once? Not necessarily. Because we are human, the result of a special creative act that fundamentally sets us apart from animals, plants, or the revolving earth, we may experience springtimes in autumn or winter. Our inner psychological abilities, and God's grace, permit us to experience springtimes more often than during just our youthful years. In fact, when we are older, we can more fully appreciate the springtimes that we experience.

We belong to two worlds at the same time. We try to express them through paired concepts like the natural and the spiritual or the physical and the psychological. Though we focus almost exclusively on the natural, physical world, the spiritual, psychological world of human existence brings us our springtimes. A life force in that dimension of human nature is always trying to break through and push us more fully into life. Spring is always trying to burst forth in us and renew us.

Many people believe that much of our inner turmoil after the age of thirty-five occurs because spring is gone forever. But that turmoil occurs because we hold back our spiritual life force. Though our sense of nostalgia wishes us back in the springtime years of youth, our need for security strongly counsels that we remain on the familiar winter ground of frozen sameness. No eruptions of new life for us! "I'm too old for that," we say. Or we excuse ourself with: "I'm too busy. I have too many other responsibilities." We'd rather stay where we are and look askance (but enviously) at the young.

But our Creator—still intent on creating us—won't let us off that easily. If we are aware of this when we read the Scriptures, we will see how often God calls us to be renewed, to blossom, and to experience more springtimes. That is precisely one of the themes of the New Testament. God, the one whose earthly springtime thrills us each year, becomes thrilled over us when we cooperate with God's grace and life force. God enthusiastically points to us and boasts: "See, I am doing something new! Now it springs forth, do you not perceive it?" (Isaiah 43:19, NAB). The psalmist rejoices as well, and reminds us that God "renews your youth like an eagle's" (Psalm 103:5, NJB). Spiritually and psychologically we are called to springtime after springtime, each one further completing us.

Do we consider ourself too old or too busy for another youthful springtime? Would we rather lament what once was than work for what still can be? Before we answer questions like these, we ought to go for a walk in the park on a warm sunny day and feel the wind blow through our hair. We ought to take a look at a couple holding hands. We ought to recapture the commitment to life we had in our youth. God often hums a favorite song on beautiful days, especially on spring days— "Everything Old Is New Again." That includes us too—especially us.

Our Personal Swampland

EACH OF US HAS AN inner self that is waiting to be born. We don't usually think of our life that way. We might say, "There's a self inside me waiting for wealth, ease, happiness, long life, and freedom." We spend our life conjugating three infinitives: to want, to have, to do. All that we accomplish by our wanting, having, and doing, however, is ultimately significant only when it is accompanied by the most fundamental infinitive—to be. Meaning and happiness consist of coming *to be* what we were made to be—an integrally developed person. Whatever is superfluous or detrimental to our *becoming* is useless or self-defeating.

We are much like a caterpillar, who is called to metamorphose by burying itself inside a cocoon only to emerge later as a butterfly. A little girl once tried to help this process of metamorphosis by using a toothpick to pry away some of the cocoon as a butterfly struggled to become itself. The butterfly died. Her dad pointed out that it needed the struggle in order to complete its transformation. Whenever a human blossoms into a newer self and flies free, she or he always leaves a husk lying in a corner somewhere.

Dr. James Hollis uses the metaphor of a swampland as the place where humans struggle to grow: "It is in the swamplands where soul is fashioned and forged, where we encounter not only the *gravitas* of life, but its purpose, its dignity and its deepest meaning."

By wrestling with life, entering the swampland of our soul, and dealing with personal inner sufferings, we attain our metamorphosis, our coming to completeness. That doesn't happen automatically. If it did, everyone who suffers would become a wonderful person. Sometimes we choose diminishment

79

because we suffer. We see ourself as a victim. Dealing positively with our problems and pain, however, serves as an occasion to tear away the cocoon of old illusions and defenses from the inside so that our true self comes out. Suffering is the prerequisite for psychological and spiritual maturation. Don't athletes sum up their physical efforts by grunting, "No pain, no gain"?

We do not seek pain for its own sake. Yet without any kind of suffering in our life, we would fail to grow. We might need to be dragged kicking and screaming into facing the difficult situations—situations that we pray God will take away—but in the end, we tap into a far greater purpose in a much bigger picture.

I write about suffering because I have counseled many people over the years, and I know we all suffer. I also try to learn from my own suffering. Our suffering is usually accompanied by resentment, as though this shouldn't be happening to us, as though suffering is a mistake when it comes. I write to remind you, and myself, that suffering is not an unnatural occurrence.

When suffering does come into our life, perhaps its effect can be minimized somewhat by understanding its larger significance. We can tolerate any *what* if we only know the *why*. All kinds of events and occurrences involving suffering are interwoven into our life. Though we will never fathom all the reasons, we can at least develop a general understanding of their place in human growth. Then, perhaps, we won't be so afraid of our personal swamplands that we miss out on all they have to offer.

Tell
Them

A MAN RECEIVED WORD that his lifelong best buddy was in a bad car accident. He rushed to the scene. On the way he thought about their early school days, their years as teammates, their double dates with their girlfriends, and the closeness of their two families now. Arriving at the crash site, he caught up with the gurney as the paramedics wheeled his severely injured friend to an ambulance. He began to cry. Then he shouted for his friend to hear: "You can't die! I haven't told you that I love you!"

Too many of us put off expressing our positive feelings for others. Whether spoken or in writing, we hesitate to verbally express our true feelings. Some feel especially inclined to do so at Christmas, birthdays, graduations, and so on, but no one time of year is better than any other. The best time is always now—now rather than later.

Why do we have such difficulty telling others what they mean to us? Why do we need an occasion to feel that it's okay to speak what is inside us, or to write a note from our heart to theirs? These are some of the causes I have discerned; each is, I think, an obstacle that can be overcome.

Vulnerability

Our feelings are part of our very core. Bringing them out into the open makes us feel vulnerable. A man explained how he felt when he spontaneously expressed tender sentiments to another adult: "It seems to me my feelings are hanging out there in the air, and I'm like a wet, needy, newborn puppy. I feel so dependent on how the other will receive my feelings, how I'll be understood. I'd feel silly and embarrassed if I cared for them

81

more than they do me, or if I risk my heart and it's not appreciated." Much is lost in life because we lack the courage to take legitimate risks.

Uneasiness with Feelings of Closeness

We all need some degree of closeness with others, but often we are uneasy about what might happen if we become very close to someone. Might we lose our self? Will the other person develop new expectations that I will not be able to fulfill? This uneasiness may cause us to keep our feelings shielded, to leave others to guess what they are.

Our Expectations of Others

Another rationale for not expressing our feelings is to expect that others should know our feelings without our needing to verbalize them. "You should know by now how I feel. Why do I have to put it into words?" Words crystallize and confirm feelings. Words show others that we accept them. Words have a special way of stroking our hearts.

Cultural Over-Associations with Sex

We have far from a healthy understanding of human sexuality in our culture. Owing to our tendency to immediately eroticize words and behavior, some people are afraid to speak fondly or appreciatively to people outside their immediate family. True expressions of caring can be misinterpreted in a culture saturated with unhealthy sexual attitudes.

And so we hesitate to tell people of our love or friendship for them. We write beautiful obituaries instead, or silently grieve for what we could have said and didn't. Too late we realize how we could have touched hearts and lifted spirits.

God must think it extremely important to communicate that we are loved. We Christians believe Christmas is all about God doing that. Sermons all year long wax eloquent with that oft-used quote, "God so loved the world, that he gave his only Son" (John 3:16). Then Jesus Christ lived his life trying to tell us that we are loved very much. You love some people very much too, don't you? Tell them! Oh, tell them!

Ten Important Things to Do Before You Die

1. Come to know and be yourself. Our whole inner person is like a pie. We are consciously aware of only a small slice of ourself. The rest is pushed out of awareness (into the unconscious) for various reasons, yet it continues to affect our feelings and behavior. To be whole and healthy, we need to get in touch with our unconscious. To accomplish that we must look into our depths to find what makes us tick; to find out why we like or dislike certain things, people, behaviors; to discover what makes us truly happy or sad; and to see who we are becoming. The best advice we can ever follow is be yourself, but be your best self.

2. Be a perpetual student in life. Stay open-minded, become aware, look for the lessons. Befriend silence and don't be afraid of new ideas and experiences. "The Truth must dazzle gradually / Or every man be blind," writes Emily Dickinson. There is so much truth yet to learn about life, God, others, and ourselves. If we cease being a student, we will miss so much and stay too small.

3. Keep the child within you alive. The older we become, the more we tend to suppress spontaneity and imagination. We become too uptight. We need to enjoy the simple things of life—go barefoot, eat more ice cream, go without an umbrella, spend more time in nature, take in a circus. We need to live in the present as much as possible so that we don't miss the beauty all around us.

4. Develop a first-circle friendship. Friendships are like the circles in a tree trunk. Most of us have friends in varying degrees of closeness, some in closer circles, others in farther ones. A first-circle friend is someone with whom we mutually and comfortably share our real self without fear of rejection or recrimination. "If in your lifetime, you find one or two such friends, consider yourself lucky," a wise teacher of mine once said. He was wise because he knew that such friends are rare and that we grow best in such genuine relationships.

5. Forgive parents, siblings, friends, others. Most of us carry around a reservoir of anger that has been formed by the still-simmering remnants of the hurts—intentional or unintentional—done to us by the important people in our life. Such anger keeps churning and gnaws away at our inner peace of mind. Sometimes we keep blaming the people who hurt us for our current unhappiness. We must forgive, let go, move on. We are responsible for ourself now.

6. Give yourself away. This does not mean that we should allow ourself to be disrespected or abused, but that we should willingly give our time, our money, our listening ear, our heart, to others who need it. We should be compassionate. We shouldn't think less *of* ourself but less *about* ourself. One of the signs of emotional maturity is finding more satisfaction in giving than in receiving.

7. Develop a deeper spiritual outlook on life. Carl Jung once said that among his patients who were in the second half of their lives, not a single one had a problem that was not related to the lack of a religious outlook on life. It is both healthy and realistic to acknowledge and deepen our relationship with God.

8. Accept your humanness. We are not perfect. We do not know everything. We cannot be liked by everyone. We will make mistakes. We will always struggle with emotions. We carry both good and evil within us. God is most patient with our slow ascent from primordial slime to eternal glory. Can't we imitate God?

9. Prefer the essential to the important. A lot of things in life are important to us, but few of them are essential. Our heart and soul will inform us of the essential; advertisers will remind us of the other. We must personally decide what is the most essential and then find the road to it. A bad bargain in life is to miss the essential for the important.

10. Find out what real love is. Nothing in the world is as essential, as saving, as healing, or as ennobling as love. If we find it, we've found all. If we miss it, we've missed everything.

Time, Don't Run Out on Me!

ADULTS HARBOR TWO BASIC illusions. One is called the rescue fantasy: Someone out there —a parent, a spouse, a benefactor, a guru— will save us from our problems and the hard responsibilities of life. Someone else will make us happy and complete.

The second illusion is immortality: We maintain a deep-seated sense of our uniqueness. Death applies to others, not to us. Sociologists observe that we are one of the most death-denying cultures ever to exist. Woody Allen spoke for most of us when he said, "It's not that I'm afraid to die; I just don't want to be there when it happens."

The wristwatches on our arms, the clocks on the wall, the calendar pages we flip, all remind us that time exists, that time is limited, that time passes away, and that time eventually comes to an end. This subliminal awareness causes an uncomfortable death anxiety that we try our best to ignore.

We resist sharp reminders that might prick the balloon of our immortality fantasy. Visiting rest homes, going to funerals, prearranging cemetery details, listening to a suspicious diagnosis—these are sure to rattle us. "White coat anxiety" even makes our blood pressure rise a bit when the doctor takes our pressure. Noticing our wrinkles, shortness of breath in climbing stairs, the ages of our children, and a host of other symptoms, all serve as those snickering intimations of mortality.

Despite all our efforts to ignore the passing of time and the approaching of death, our birthday comes along and we begrudgingly celebrate amid jokes of loss and aging. And now we've entered a new millennium. The changing of four digits from 1999 to 2000 led some to conclude that the world would end, that computer failures would cause major catastrophes, and that space invaders would finally arrive. Rather than seeing the passing of time as a positive occurrence, some saw it as something that would destroy our wealth, security, and existence.

Our fears and illusions about birthdays and the new millennium are examples of our death anxiety. Death anxiety is both neurotic and normal; we all experience it. But some of us experience such excessive amounts that it spills over and constricts growth, spontaneity, and the life God has given us to live fully. Neurotic anxiety causes us to live dedicated to safety, survival, and a denial that motivates us to a superficial and hectic life pace. We run away from time. We become hypochondriacal and fear the illness and suffering that reveal our mortality.

A person best faces inevitable death when he or she has had the experience of fully living. Death anxiety is inversely proportional to life satisfaction. Jesus Christ knew and taught that life is to be *lived:* "I came that they may have life, and have it abundantly" (John 10:10). Our call is to life, not to numbness.

Paradoxically death makes a positive contribution to life involvement and awareness though it takes most of us a long time to understand the paradox. The limited nature of time makes it so precious, just as the limited amount of gold or diamonds makes them so valuable. Acceptance of death is a catalyst that plunges us into life more authentically. The emphasis is on authentic life modes—those achieved through love and intimacy, through altruistic caring and service—not the inauthentic modes of hedonism and self-centeredness that express resistance to death and that empty life of all expansiveness and fulfillment.

Time does not run out on us, but we can run out on time if we refuse to live intensely, to love deeply, or to grow expansively. We can run out on time if we refuse the gift, close our doors, and pull the blinds. Accepting the gift of time from God at the door is crucially important. As Henri Boulad points out: "Human beings choose themselves, and time is the sphere in which they have the possibility of making this choice. In this sense we call time creative, since it is to time that human beings owe the possibility of becoming and shaping themselves." The irreversibility of time is not a catastrophe, but it gives great importance to how we live and what we choose. We are the clay, and God is the potter; and time is the clay, and we are the potter. We are to be engaged in the same wonderful work as God.

We Have Met the Enemy, and It Is Us

I HAVE A FRAMED COPY of the late Walt Kelly's comic strip character Pogo. Pogo, standing in a rowboat looking at his reflection in the water, peers in and says, "We has met the enemy, and it is us." Poor grammar but excellent insight. We are our own worst enemy, though we rarely realize that fact. We are responsible for our happiness or unhappiness, but we like to blame others.

That is a hard truth to accept. But to make our life any better, we must accept it sooner or later. Reality neither has it in for us nor does it take our side. How we interpret reality is what matters, and this interpretation has its basis in our inner world. Help or hindrance may come to us from others, but the most essential help or hindrance comes from inside ourself. Our true adversaries are not objective facts—not the fact I was born to poor parents, had little money, or didn't go to college. Our true enemies are ourself and our interpretation of the facts and occurrences of our life—and what we choose to do about them. To develop psychologically and spiritually, we must maintain a certain objectivity within external situations, and we must not give situations total control. We must know ourself *in light* of the situations, not *as* the situations. We have no control over these situations, but only over how we react to them.

Take, for example, two boys who grew up with an alcoholic father. As adult men one of these boys became an alcoholic himself and experienced a troubled life similar to his dad's. The other boy became a man who completely abstained from drugs and alcohol, developed a fulfilling family life, and did well in business. If you asked the alcoholic why his life was so problematic, he would reply, "My dad was an alcoholic, and his example had such an influence on me that I developed the same problem." If you asked the other man why his life was healthy and successful, he would say, "My dad was an alcoholic, and because of his example and the pain it caused, I decided I had to expend a lot of effort so that I wouldn't end up that way too."

As children our life is affected by the external factors around us—an alcoholic parent, poverty, wealth. Those factors begin to form attitudes, reactions, and behaviors that become embedded in us. Maturity is characterized by our becoming more aware of these external factors and learning to evaluate our life and recognize our ability to choose differently.

One of these brothers didn't let the external factors of his childhood influence his life choices, and the other did. One evaluated the results of his father's addiction and deliberately chose a different direction for himself. The other avoided that essential interior work, saw himself as a victim. One was willing to put forth the effort to understand both the external world of his family situation and his own unconscious world that offered the freedom to choose otherwise. The other didn't care to spend the time or effort. He did not wish to meet the real enemy—himself, not his father. Being a victim of some other enemy appeals to many of us. It gains us sympathy and provides excuses. It gave the alcoholic brother a way to sidestep the growth that was possible for him.

By human nature we tend to dread becoming more conscious ourself. This is why denial holds such sway in our life, why we can only stand a bit of reality at a time. Most of us prefer to remain unconscious and drift along in the current created by the external factors of our lives. We complain about that current, about the people we think cause the current, and about our own sad state. Real freedom comes the day we learn to swim upstream. It comes the day we study our reflection in the water and say with Pogo, "We have met the enemy, and he is us." It is freeing, because if we know we are our own enemy, then we have options. We are not in prison. We can do something about it.

Believing in ourself is a daring risk to take. It is scary and causes anxiety, but it is delicious. When we believe in ourself, we step out, unsupported, into psychic space where we have never dared to go before. We travel into new territory. "Lord! we know what we are, but know not what we may be," Shakespeare wrote in *Hamlet*. Conquering our inner enemies permits us to find out what we can be.

Greed in a Land of Stocks, Glitz, and Nutrasweet

AS FAR BACK AS the sixth century, Pope Saint Gregory the Great saw that all our various vices and personal sins flow from seven chief sources, or heads (*caput* is Latin for "head"). He termed these seven sources the seven *capital sins*—pride, envy, anger, sloth, lust, greed, and gluttony.

Each of the capital sins deals with something good and natural that is sought excessively. For example, it is critically important that we think well of ourself. Self-esteem becomes pride when we excessively focus on ourself to the exclusion of concern and compassion for others. Food and drink are good and necessary for life. Gluttony occurs when we become unreasonably obsessed with eating and drinking.

We all need material possessions to survive and plan for the future. Greed is the *inordinate* love of money and material possessions, and the dedication of oneself to their pursuit. Greed is seldom spoken of negatively today. It has been inverted and given a good spin, to the extent that the pursuit of wealth is a dominant value in our society. So how can we condemn it? Those of us who chase wealth inordinately are praised. We are hailed as bright, ambitious, successful. The media feature stories of thirty-year-old multi-millionaires. What is not discussed is whether such goals are commendable, or at what psychological or spiritual costs they have been achieved. Were immoral means used to accumulate this wealth? What good for others will come from the wealth of this one person?

Greed is considered a capital sin because of what it does to us and to others. A common syndrome seen by therapists is the material-driven executive who is so preoccupied with amassing wealth that in the process he destroys his health, his relationships, and his values, and is desensitized to the sufferings of those who are poor. Jesus' question, "What will it profit them to gain the whole world and forfeit their life?" (Mark 8:36), is still valid.

A spiritual director said to a group of clergy: "There are many wealthy who need you today. They thought that when they possessed a lot they would be happy. The truth is that many of them are beginning to suffer an inner depression and emptiness. They are now more open to seek the true riches of love, relationship, and a solid spiritual faith." Think of the story of Midas. He thought he would be successful and wealthy when everything he touched turned to gold. Instead Midas lost much more than he gained. We can too. If we become more and more preoccupied with evaluating life and all things in terms of golden monetary worth, we will lose the ability to see things for what they really are. People, relationships, actions, and time are all coated with economic value to a Midas. "How can this person help me get ahead?" "What can I get from him or her?" "What can I sell them?"

Considering greed ought not be an occasion for disdaining all wealthy people. It is possible to have wealth and still keep God, others, and our soul in perspective. It is just more difficult. Neither Aristotle nor Aquinas condemned the desire for material things per se. Only the failure of moderation in this desire is spoken of as a vice or sin.

The Gospel of John relates an eye-opening fact about Jesus Christ. In preparation for his crucifixion, the soldiers stripped Jesus of a seamless robe he was wearing. Because it was not a patchwork of individual pieces sewn together—as were most robes in those days—it could not be easily disassembled. It was such a fine robe, a Brooks Brothers robe, that the soldiers decided to throw dice for it rather than cut it apart. Did the possession of something so expensive make Christ, the wearer, uncaring for the poor? His life and actions proved otherwise. His openness to and love of others, his active concern for the poor, sick, and alienated, were his chief preoccupations. His behavior, not his clothes, showed where his heart was. In the third millennium since his birth, we will continue to live in a culture surrounded by wealth, enticing commercials, and a materialistic spirit that tells us that having more is all we need to be happy. But greed remains one of the seven capital sins. In the face of our culture's dominant value, we do well to pray, "Lead us not into temptation."

How Can I Hear God's Voice?

> I find myself in somewhat of a predicament for fifty-eight years of age. My life's aim now is to carry out the will of God as best I can. Everywhere I turn I'm directed to 'Listen! Listen!' I wonder—listen to what? I thought at this age I would hear God more clearly. I don't. What will make the voice of God's directing Spirit more audible?
> Signed, Francine.

Dear Francine, it is difficult, isn't it? We either don't hear any discernible voice at all, or we hear so many competing voices that we have difficulty perceiving which is authentic. No wonder we say that the tolerance of ambiguity is one of the signs of maturity.

Francine, will I disappoint you if I have no pat answer to give you? The same struggle you go through, I go through, and indeed so do most people. The Ten Commandments and the Beatitudes are of immense help in directing our lives according to God's will. Yet their application and interpretation to the unique and complex problems of our individual lives puzzle us. We yearn for a guru to tell us, we call out for God's voice, we look for signs telling us what to do. When others ask my advice, I know I cannot always give an exact answer that solves everything, but I can respond to you—questions and response, not questions and answers, for what I say may or may not be answer enough for you.

Your search for clear direction leads you to feel like you are in a predicament. It sounds like you are right where you should be. The latter half of life is when psyche and Spirit do their stirring. They prod us to take an interest

91

in our own life. Their task is to lead us to wholeness and truth. They get our attention by causing anxiety or emptiness. Our accumulated wisdom urges us to discover where these feelings came from. Though you seek a more audible voice, one more definite, I would instead offer you the advice given by Austrian poet Rainer Maria Rilke:

> Have patience with everything unresolved in your heart and try to love *the questions themselves* as if they were locked rooms or books written in a very foreign language. Don't search for the answers. . . . *Live* the questions now. Perhaps then, someday far in the future, you will gradually, without even noticing it, live your way into the answer.

That's unwelcome advice when we want answers right now, when we find the challenges of life too daunting, when the path we walk has too many forks from which we must choose. But Rilke calls on us to live life rather than be handed it, to be open rather than see immediate closure. That gives us and God's grace enough time to do their work. Rather than get answers from a book or a thunderous voice, Rilke urges us to ferret them out every day, to live our way into the answers. That's the same advice we give our children, isn't it? We don't just tell them about life and consider that enough. As they grow up, we offer them sound words of specific advice, but we offer them more—love, respect, and the freedom to meet divergent paths and choose responsibly for themselves. Everyone must be given the chance to make his or her own mistakes. We recognize the voice of God more convincingly after mistakes.

I also urge you, Francine, to know yourself better. A spark of divinity is buried within you. Find it and listen to it. Psychological and spiritual attention help us do that. True psychology is intertwined with true spirituality; they are not opposed. The three places we can come to know ourself the best are marriage, psychotherapy, and silence. If we can be honest and face our real inner self in one or all of these three places, answers slowly rise to the surface of our awareness.

Francine, I admire your desire to become a better person. Remember, however, our goal isn't perfection but completeness. Of course, completeness is an ideal too, and it is no more reachable than perfection. But as Carl Jung put it, "The goal is important only as an idea; the essential thing is the *opus* [that's the work on yourself] which leads to the goal: *that* is the goal of a lifetime."

The Long Bag We Drag Behind Us

THE VARIOUS PARTS that make up our person are very intriguing. Who are we more interested in than ourself? Knowing about ourself is conducive to our development, helping us cope more effectively with the problems of life. Ignorance of ourself increases our problems.

Author Robert Bly has an engaging book called *A Little Book on the Human Shadow.* What part of us is called our shadow? Is it the dark silhouette behind us when we face the sun? In Jungian psychology the shadow means much more. Let's try to understand our shadow with the help of Robert Bly's imagery.

When we were very young, we were like a globe of active energy. We had a 360-degree personality. But there soon came days when we began to notice that our parents didn't like certain parts of our globe. They said things like, "Stop jumping so much, and sit still!" Or, "It isn't nice to throw stones at your brother like that."

Behind us we have an invisible bag. We took the parts of ourself that our parents didn't approve of, and, in order to keep their love, we put those parts inside the bag. By the time we went to school, our bag was rather large. Then our teachers said things to us: "Good children don't become angry over such little things." So we took some of our anger and put it in the bag. By doing so we were praised as "nice" boys and girls.

In high school we did a lot more bag stuffing. Only this time it wasn't those terrible adults who pressured us. Our peers did. We wanted so desperately to be popular, cool, "with it." Any thing or behavior that was not in fashion went in the bag.

When we reached our twenties, we had only a slice left of our original 360-degree globe of energy. The rest was in the bag. But some of it needs to be there in order to live together and form a society. We can't carry out all our natural impulses. We can't throw toys to hurt another. We can't punch or kick or steal or intrude on others' rights or space.

Unfortunately along with the things we *need* to put into the bag goes a lot of creativity, spontaneity, and individuality. The good things about ourself that we put away make up the golden part of our shadow. Until we are twenty or thirty, we spend our life deciding which parts of ourself to put into the bag. Then, somewhere in the middle of life, we try to discover which parts to let back out of the bag.

This can be frustrating and even painful, but it must be done. We don't easily bring things out again because we risk censure, even rejection. We are also afraid of the power of the feelings we've put there, afraid of our potential for both good and evil. Many of us settle for remaining the nice boy or girl we've always been. We're afraid to change even in the interest of growth. So we keep the anxiety resulting from the unanswered call within us, and forego the labor pains that would have delivered a better self. Personal growth is too scary.

The most freeing thing we can do for ourself in the second half of life, which Jung says is age thirty-five and older, is to find out who we really are. We can do this only by exploring our shadow, which represents everything that has been repressed or has gone unrecognized. Of course, the bag is not behind us but is deep within us. The shadow contains all that is vital yet problematic—anger, sexuality, joy, spontaneity, and untapped creative resources. In the second half of life, we experience a strong call to know ourself and to become more authentic, to become the unique being that God has made us to be. We are called to become our true self, not to remain contrived or false.

One of our dearest and more basic needs is security. We like to stay as we are and avoid change. But knowing our shadow induces us to change. Evil seeks darkness in which to hide; consciousness and self-honesty seek light. By opening the bag, we find three things: our real unique self, our commonness with others, and the great God of Life, whose stamp is on our person. What surprises!

Mountain Climbing

HE CAME TO MY OFFICE to keep an appointment he had requested. A man in his late fifties, he was having a variety of problems. Both he and his wife were experiencing health problems, but he was especially concerned about the problems in the lives of his grown children—the kinds of problems parents would like to carry for their children but can only worry about.

Though he smiled politely, his sense of disappointment was obvious. He said: "You know, Father Lou, I've always thought that if you worked hard at handling life when you were younger, things would eventually get better. To me life is like climbing a mountain. I've always had the expectation that by this time in my life I would come to a kind of plateau where the troubles of life level off. Now I'm beginning to wonder if there is a plateau. The mountain just keeps going up— and I'm getting so tired of climbing."

I had known this man for some time. He was a true, conscientious gentleman. This was one of the times when I, as do many clergy, wished I had a special word or prayer to solve someone's heartache. I realize, however, that all I have is the same humanness and a listening ear.

"As a mountain climber, what are your options?" I inquired.

"Well," he mused, "I guess I could just sit still and cry and wait for someone else to help me, or I could slide down to the bottom and stop climbing. Then again I could give up and jump off the mountain and end all the climbing." After a long, thoughtful pause, he suggested, "Or—I can keep climbing."

You can tell in people's voices, faces, and eyes when they have arrived at their own

95

convincing solution, when they have come to an answer that is *really* the answer—not just an escape or an expected reply. This was one of those times. He realized that the true solution, which called for much courage, was just to keep on keeping on.

I asked him what benefit he, or any of us, could expect if we keep climbing the mountain in difficult times. He paused and looked away for a moment, as though he didn't quite know how it could benefit us. Then he knew! He looked me in the eye, smiled, and resolutely said, "When you keep on climbing, the view gets better."

Before me sat a very wise man. A man becoming wiser, a man gaining insight into himself and into many of the perplexing paradoxes of life. He realized that his continued climb up the mountain of life may or may not find him a plateau upon which to rest. But it would gain him a height from which to find meaning, a view.

After all, that's what we're really looking for. Sometimes we suppose that what we're looking for is blissful comfort. No! Our pet cats or dogs can do that as they snooze in the sunshine. We have a life to form, a mind that seeks understanding, and a heart with which to learn love. We want a bigger view to tell us what life's all about.

Life is not a disease, not a picnic or a punishment. It is a path by which to travel somewhere. The wise man's metaphor was perfect. Life is not meant to be a smooth amusement park water chute on which we slide effortlessly into warm, womblike security. Life is more like climbing a mountain. We are not expected to lay back and glide; we are expected to climb. The climb may be hard for us at times, but the view becomes more revealing as we go, inviting us to a broader, fuller understanding of our experience.

I have fond memories of climbing mountains with family and friends in Colorado. When we climb we arrive at places where we feel surrounded by a silence that is almost tangible. The air is pure, the sun is bright, and we must stop and look out. Talk about perspective! Talk about a view! We feel humbled and small, yet part of a mighty creation. The events of life take on a new perspective. Someone once remarked, "When you climb a mountain, you feel like you're meeting God halfway."

The One I Love Is Not Enough

SOME MARRIAGES END because of great mistakes. Spouses consciously or unconsciously deceive themselves. They married under the influence of some illusion or infatuation, or to escape an unpleasant home situation, or they were not mature enough to know the meanings of genuine love. Later they realize the gravity of their mistake. Clergy and counselors strive to help such couples see reality before their wedding takes place. Unfortunately when we believe we are *in* love, we are often *out* of reason.

We laugh at the naiveté of couples in the past who thought that merely having a wedding ceremony enabled them to live happily ever after. But before we laugh too loudly, are we sure we don't still harbor naiveté? We may not believe that the wedding ceremony guarantees a utopia, but what about the more subtle expectation that just having a romantic relationship will guarantee the same thing? When some years pass, and the romance and passion seem to fade, don't we become disillusioned? Don't we conclude that the whole marriage is wrong and proceed toward divorce? "It will be easier with someone new." "I'm married to the wrong person." "The thrill is gone, and that means the marriage is gone." These conclusions are, for the most part, too quickly reached.

Such diagnoses are usually built on an unrealistic grasp of human nature. Spouses who believe them are often unaware of what is called the transcendence of longing. If we believe that perfect happiness comes with having that which we most desire, then having whatever or whoever we long for will always lead to disappointment. Our longing always goes beyond what is finite. We should

97

have started learning this lesson when childhood toys, greatly anticipated, became tiresome; we should have learned it when we realized that our hunger for more and more possessions is never satisfied. When two people promise each other perfect contentment, perfect love, they promise something that only God can give.

That will always be true, because what we really are looking for is God. There is a certain kind of infinity in our dream of love. When we marry we consider our spouse an advance agent of heaven. "He or she will make me completely happy." The truth is, our longings will always go beyond the other person, and the other person's longing will always go beyond us. Every bride is half woman and half dream; every groom is half man and half dream. No one person, no series of affairs with others, will satisfy the hungers of our heart.

Understanding the transcendence of longing is critically important. By acknowledging it we can build relationships that last. We can grow closer and closer to one another, and in so doing receive immense satisfaction, but that satisfaction always leaves room for much more. Love beckons two people to come to it, but never permits itself to be fully possessed in this world. The best is always ahead. The road goes ever on and on.

A real relationship springs from a conscious desire to share the journey with another human being, and to grow nearer to the mystery of love through the bridges of conversation, sexuality, and compassion. As we take the hand of that imperfect human beside us, we learn of our own imperfect humanness, and haltingly lead each other toward the One who is Love.

"You'll never be able to love God unless you first love someone with skin on," said an old preacher. The Scriptures also inform us of the difficulty of loving a God we can't see if we can't learn to love those we *can* see. Many a husband or wife, after many years of living and growing in a healthy relationship, have been heard to say: "When we got married, I thought that I loved my wife (or my husband) so much that I would not be able to love more. Now I know that that sentiment was nothing compared to the love I have today." That's a realistic attitude, one attuned to the transcendence of longing.

Though the one I love is not enough, the one I love can introduce me to heaven. If God did not permit this preview of joy, who would venture beyond the vestibule?

Trying to Be Perfect People

IMMEDIATELY AFTER BIRTH, along with sentiments of love and joy, someone ought to whisper in our ear, "Nobody's perfect." That might offset the pet gargoyle that will soon accompany us through life. Yes, riding on the shoulder of most human beings is an ugly, invisible gargoyle. Throughout life he points out every slip-up, mistake, or faux pas. His name is perfectionism. He's never completely pleased with us, and he tells us that we must do better if we plan to be accepted by parents, by God, and by others. As he speaks he reminds us that we have a blemish on our face and that our wrists are too fat.

Because of him we can receive ten compliments and one negative criticism and remember only the criticism. We can type ten thousand words flawlessly and misspell two, and we're irked by those two. We make a dumb statement to our boss, and we're mortified. We expect to be gods or angels, not humans. We try to be perfect people. Because we want to be perfect, we have a hard time saying, "I was wrong," "I don't know," or "I apologize."

Organized religion must guard against being the gargoyle's collaborator. If God's love for us is conditioned on perfection, it is not love at all. It is then an earned reward, and love is not earned—it is given. Observe how often preachers imply that unless we do everything right and love God first, God will withhold love from us. Some clergy emphasize Matthew 5:48, "Be perfect therefore, as your heavenly Father is perfect," not realizing that with these words Jesus is calling us to become whole, loving humans rather than demanding that we do everything perfectly right. A friend laughingly told me of his dream about not being perfect: "I had a nightmare the other night. I had died and was in line waiting to get into heaven. I discovered that Mother Teresa was standing in line in front of me. She got to the front of the line, God paged through his book, looked at her and said, 'You didn't do enough!' Wow! I started to sweat—and then I woke up."

Once perfectionism gets a grip on us, it is hard to shake, though we try all sorts of escapes. Some of us get so tired of constantly trying to be perfect that we unconsciously mess up so as to take the pressure off and convince ourself and others that we're no good so that we can stop trying. Other people try to appear perfect by pointing out the faults of others or making fun of their defects. Still others think they can actually satisfy the gargoyle. They submit to the illusion of perfection and try to become perfect. They run faster, do more, take a long time to make decisions, and watch every step. But the gargoyle of perfectionism is a slave driver who rides us unmercifully and always tells us that we haven't done enough. Perfectionism eventually wears us down.

The healthiest escape from the compulsion of perfectionism is humility—remembering who we are. We are human, a condition succinctly described by Ernest Kurtz and Katherine Ketcham: "To be human is to be incomplete, yet yearn for completion; it is to be uncertain, yet long for certainty; to be imperfect, yet long for perfection; to be broken, yet crave wholeness." We want so badly to be God, to be all perfect, but we are not. We need to learn to accept, humbly, that our yearnings will go unfulfilled.

In one way it's a great relief to realize we're imperfect humans, capable of mistakes of all sizes and magnitudes. This realization shows us who we are and who God is, and it compels us to pray for help. The most basic prayer of a human has two words addressed to God: "Help me!" For over a thousand years in monasteries where the Psalms are prayed daily, each monastic hour of the day begins with the words from Psalm 70: "Be pleased, O God, to deliver me. O Lord, make haste to help me!"

Do you ever feel the bite of imperfection? Do you have a gargoyle on your shoulder whispering criticisms? Do you fear the possibility of making more mistakes as you age? God holds out to us the priceless gift of unconditional love. God's love is not based on our perfection or anything we do or anything we have or have not done. God unexplainably gives us love because that's the way God is. God smiles out of love for us. It's worth being imperfect just to discover that!

Placebos and the Powers Within Us

FOR A STUDY ON allergies, two hundred people were given a pill to take daily. They recorded symptoms and side effects in a journal, and after a month each person was tested for the effectiveness of the medication.

Placebos are an integral part of such research. A placebo—from the Latin meaning "I shall please (you)"—is an imitation medicine, given to please the patient. A placebo has no medicine in it at all. It is a milk or sugar tablet dressed up like medicine. In research studies placebos are given to some of the people involved, and the actual medicine is given to the others. Neither group knows which has the real medicine.

The amazing fact is that many people are relieved of pain, disease, and discomfort by placebos. We accomplish healing ourself by our mind and body. How placebos work is not exactly known, but that they work is beyond doubt. The power of the placebo seems not to be that it fools the body, but that it affects the mind, and the mind affects the body. The placebo serves as a catalyst for psychological factors that translate the will to live into a physical reality. Placebos can eventually trigger specific biochemical changes in the body.

Placebo power—mental power—does not encourage us to avoid doctors, medicines, or operations, which are often extremely necessary. But placebos help us realize that what goes on within us psychologically and spiritually is also important. Our will to live, our awareness of what is within us, and our hope and insights into fears and anxieties are critically important as well. Current studies indicate how one's faith life, prayer, touch, and so on, also play a part in the healing process. Even mood and laughter.

We often belittle the psychological and spiritual areas of life. Some scientifically macho attitudes consider them to be inconsequential or childish. Attitudes like those sometimes spring from the bias of the secular world against the unquantifiable areas of human life, like religion and psychology, or from the general fear we have of the psychological world within.

Sophisticated people may believe that their higher educational status places them beyond the effect of placebos. Contrary to common perceptions, research points out that the higher a person's intelligence, the greater the potential benefit from the use of placebos.

The vast majority of us fear and avoid our own inner psychological lives. So a major part of the placebo's effectiveness comes from the fact that it plays along with us yet reveals our error. It preserves our illusion at first. In a sense it says to us, "Here is some new medicine that will help you." It goes along with our illusion that all help comes from outside us. The placebo, after all, is actually something outside us that we take within. It has size and shape. We can hold it in our hand and feel it. It satisfies our craving for something external and tangible and scientific. It participates in one of our most basic illusions—the rescue fantasy that there will always be someone or something outside us to save us.

Placebos reveal how wrong we are. Their success depends on the power of the psychological and spiritual areas within. The prescriptions we write for ourself to gain health, as well as happiness and meaning, seldom contain attention to our soul and psyche. The opposite of what we think may often be the key to our health and peace. That is a more aware, inner, and simple life.

Our life is significantly affected when we permit the spiritual part of ourself to go undeveloped, and when we resist psychological searching. Think what could happen if we could effect what a placebo effects without taking it! The power of the placebo reminds us that the Divine Physician resides within to help us and to help us help ourself.

Rigid People

CABLE TELEVISION CARRIES several religious programs. I can watch them only for a short time because I begin to feel sad, angry, and uncomfortable. Why? Because I believe the God of all existence is more freeing, compassionate, mysterious, and beautiful than the God I see presented. Many who speak for God strike me as rigid people.

Rigid people can't live with doubt. They have to feel that they have all the answers. Fr. John Powell says:

> Rigid people . . . need to complete their pictures in a hurry. So they put together only a few of the pieces in a small and tight pattern. These pieces are all they need. More pieces would only confuse them. . . . To hear such people talk, they would appear to have more certainties than anyone else.

Realistic people know that God's ways are beyond our ways. They take the pieces they have and accept new pieces into the whole picture as they mature. Rigid people are like detectives who take the first few clues they find to solve a mystery. If new evidence comes up, they bend it to fit their original perceptions. Rigid people fear change because they fear that if they change, they will lose the little that they have.

Rigid people think they have God under their control. They like to feel special, and they like to call the plays. They think that if they say certain prayers or act a particular way, they can make happen what they want to happen. A healer once boasted that God had been healing a lot of diabetes problems through him the last two weeks. I didn't know God had specials of the week! And aren't our sufferings sometimes hidden blessings we must keep?

Rigid religious people tend to live and to motivate by fear. Once I saw a Catholic priest on television who dissuaded fellow Catholics from attending the wedding reception of their friend because it was an unapproved second marriage. "No way!" he said. "Why sing and dance with people on their way to hell?" Wow! Wouldn't you feel kinda silly, Father, if God was planning to attend that reception? Maybe God knows things you don't know about the inner lives of that couple.

I believe that I hear God's voice more authentically in the words of priest, author, and psychologist Fr. Adrian van Kaam. He says:

> The religious person who strives after perfection may be sometimes rigid not only in his orientation but also in his behavior. At such times he refuses to pay attention to his own feelings and to the feelings of others. . . . He is the essence of determination, and he makes many people, most of all himself, unhappy because he does not respect the sensitivity of the human heart. He is like a taut wire of will power.

Yes, I know the psalmist says that "the fear of the Lord is the beginning of wisdom" (Psalm 111:10). We can't overlook the word *beginning* in that statement. As children we have a healthy fear of our parents, but if we grow, that fear is replaced by love and trust. The same is true for our relationship with God. Spiritual infants fear God. The spiritually mature trust in God's love and forgiveness.

Rigid religious people often seem afraid of human joys. Emotionalism runs rampant in some religious television programs. But that is not joy; that is inflamed transient excitement. On the other hand, other religious broadcasts reek of dry dogmatism, devoid of humanness and joy. They subtly suggest that we are to distrust the joys of human existence, that God holds joy suspect. H. L. Mencken provided a pointed definition of Puritanism: "The haunting fear that someone, somewhere, may be happy." Remnants of Catholic Jansenism and Protestant Puritanism unfortunately still survive.

Our soul constantly hungers to know the presence and love of the God ever ancient and ever new. What an excellent opportunity the media provide. Yet from what I see and hear as I wield my remote, most of our churches are missing the opportunity.

Rules for Being Human

1. You will receive a body. You may like it or hate it, but it will be yours for your entire period here. If you expect others to respect it, you must respect it. If you treat it well, it will treat you well. How it looks is not as important as who you are.

2. The human mind is meant to know, to understand, and to learn lessons. You are already enrolled in a full-time informal school called Life. Each day you will have the opportunity to learn more lessons and to grow. Those who learn and grow become mature and wise. Those who don't, find that their body surpasses their mind. Don't flunk life!

3. Especially treasure your heart and its feelings. About feelings: You can't just sort out and keep the pleasant feelings and banish the painful feelings. They all exist together like the colors of the rainbow. Either they all come into your life, or they all stay out. If you try to keep all feelings out of your heart, then no person will come in either, nor will love, nor will life.

4. There are no mistakes, only lessons. You are made to grow into what you can be, and growth is a process of trial and error, risks and experimentation. The pains of failed experiments are as much a part of the process as are the joys of the experiments that are successful; usually they are more important. A lesson will be repeated in various forms until you learn it. When you have learned it, you can go on to the next lesson. Learning lessons does not end. You are always a student.

5. "There" is no better than "here," though the best situation always seems to be happening "there." So you try to get "there." When you do get to a "there" and it becomes a "here," you will yearn for another "there" that will inevitably look better again than "here." Always appreciate the "here."

6. Others are often seen as mirrors of you. You cannot strongly love or hate something about another person unless it reflects unconsciously to you something you love or hate about yourself. Notice what you feel strongly about in others.

7. Don't be afraid to believe. Believing in what you can't prove—God, love, the future—stretches the walls of your soul and lets you peek over the horizon of sight. Reality is much more than you can see. Believing leads to wonderful surprises.

8. What you make of your life is up to you. You have all the tools and resources you need in your mind, heart, soul, and body. The attitudes you form spring entirely from the thoughts you choose to keep in mind. The integrity you develop comes from what you choose to do or not do, the omissions and commissions of your life. No one can exercise for you. No one can choose for you.

9. The answers to life's questions lie inside you. All you need to do is take the time and effort to look, listen, and understand deeply enough. To do that you must become a friend of silence and reflection. An old woman expressed the source of her wisdom very well when she said, "All my teachers are dead now, except silence."

10. In the most essential things of life, you will eventually get what you want. If you really want love, you will find love; if you wish to exist alone, you will exist alone; if you want material possessions, you will get them. Be careful about what you want most of all. You will get it. You may not get what you ask for, but you will get what you really want.

In Praise of Silence

WHY DO WE DISLIKE silence so much? One reason is that we fear looking at all that is within us. We are masters at avoiding confrontation with who we really are. Notice the ways we avoid silence: we listen to others' thoughts on radio or television, we surf the Internet, we absorb ourself in cell phones and laptops, we click on keyboards, we talk, and we talk some more. We wake up with sound and music and go to bed the same way. Interestingly we can even busy ourself with saying rote or hurried prayers to avoid the real silence in which we might see ourself or hear the voice of God. We make ourself too busy to be silent, afraid of what we might hear and see.

Our fear of death is another reason we dislike silence. Utter silence can remind us of death. When we cease doing something so fundamentally human as using words for self-expression, we at first experience a kind of self-annihilation. Talking, working, humming, fidgeting, and listening seem to confirm our existence. Our activity proves we are here and alive.

Silence does not mean death, however. Silence can lead to more life, growth, wisdom, and healing. The good analyst and the wise spiritual teacher always encourage periods of silence. We have within us a core center of stillness that is surrounded by silence. In this center place, we find our true self. But we often feel discomfort in that silence; words fail us there, and we feel lost and frightened in that inexpressible world.

But we can work our way through the scary part of silence that agitates us. We then come to an inner place where the quality of silence changes. There we are the most with

107

ourself and God. When two people genuinely love each other, don't they often communicate without words? Times of shared silence often are concentrated moments of communion between lovers. Silence can become comforting; solitude is not loneliness. The apparently empty place of silence is actually indescribably full.

Yes, we have to go through the frightening silence to reach the eloquent silence. Only then do we begin to discover that eloquent silence is not an absence but a presence, not boring but refreshing. Eloquent silence is that enchanted place where space is cleared, time subsides, and the horizon expands. Pico Iyer puts it well:

> In silence, we often say, we can hear ourself think; but what is truer to say is that in silence we can hear ourself not think, and so sink below our selves into a place far deeper than mere thought allows. In silence, we might better say, we can hear someone else think.

The one we can hear is God. In this world we need desperately to connect with God, and God is not heard in noise and restlessness. Silence is the tribute we pay to holiness, to mystery. Some religions slip off their shoes as they enter a holy place. Perhaps we ought to slip off words. If noise is the theme song of this world, silence permits us to hear the music of the other world. Mystery cannot be imprisoned by our words, wrapped in sound, or confined to this world. It flees from noise, slips out of syllables, eludes the book of dogmas. Like a flirtation, the mystery of our beautiful God reveals itself in short glimpses during the personal stillness of silence.

Starved for Reasons, but We Won't Eat

NO PEOPLE IN HISTORY have dealt with the complexities we deal with—suicide, chemical warfare, surrogate motherhood, genetic engineering, cyber-pornography, abortion, ethnic cleansing, homosexual marriage, cloning, euthanasia, child murder, and a host of other dilemmas, tragedies, and problems.

We are starved for better understanding to help us cope, but we don't make our way to the banquet table of wisdom and eat. We eat from our own brown paper bags, our hastily prepared snacks and routine sandwiches.

As rational beings we are innately nudged to make sense of all we experience. We reach conclusions, act on them, teach them to our children, and decide what to welcome into society for the common good. But how equipped are we to form solid conclusions on the complicated issues of our day? How able are we to form not just pragmatic solutions but moral conclusions on the rightness or wrongness of issues all around us?

Narcissism and simplistic thinking are the sources of too many solutions today. Conventional wisdom is considered authentic by large segments of our population. Self-centered principles are employed to answer huge dilemmas: "If I am able to do it, and I want to do it, it's okay for me to do it." That logic covers any "it," whether the "it" is to smoke, use drugs, get drunk, use chemical warfare, have an extramarital affair, pollute the environment, publish sex on the Internet, or help an aged, depressed relative end his or her life.

Additional reasons confirming our conclusions, and substituting for thinking include, "Nobody gets hurt," "It's my right," "The polls show that most people say," and

"Everybody else is doing it." Currently many important societal institutions are failing to teach or demonstrate how to think well. More often than not, the family, school, church, and mass media are deficient in guiding us in solid thinking. Instead of being encouraged to think for ourself, we are encouraged to obey, to be safe, to develop esteem, or to tune in to the spin doctors.

Thankfully a few voices urge us to think. M. Scott Peck, MD, acknowledges both the necessity for thinking today and the difficult nature of the task:

> Thinking is difficult. Thinking is complex. And thinking is—more than anything else—a process, with a course or direction, a lapse of time, and a series of steps or stages that lead to some result. . . . If we are to think well, we must be on guard against simplistic thinking in our approach to analyzing crucial issues and solving the problems of life.

No wonder many of us sense that we are ill-prepared to form moral conclusions about complex issues. Most of us adults ended any serious religious education in our teens or college years—if we received any then. And if we did, we remember much of it as simplistic memorization of facts, dogmas, or Bible stories. Questioning was not encouraged, and the answers were given, but the thinking processes that led to the answers were neglected. For the rest of our life, we will base moral conclusions on what we learned as a child, or we will abdicate our responsibility to others who may be equally untrained.

Masters of manipulation take advantage of our limitations by using slogans and sound bites to appeal to our feelings, thus circumventing the thought process altogether. Many people felt good about slavery. Church officials felt good about the Inquisition. Hitler's speeches convinced the people that the cause of Germany's problems was the Jews.

Are today's complexities to be decided by feeling or thinking? Challenging times call for more responsibility. How often do we read solid and constructive books on issues of our day? If our church, synagogue, or community offers competent speakers on contemporary topics, how often do we attend?

"It was the best of times, it was the worst of times, it was the age of wisdom, it was the age of foolishness, it was the epoch of belief, it was the epoch of incredulity." So wrote Charles Dickens as he began his novel *A Tale of Two Cities*. Sounds applicable today, doesn't it?

Take
Time
to
Live

SOME EQUATE LIFE with just being here. But that's not *living,* that's existing. Just being here is a situation shared by rocks, sequoias, and kumquats. Existing is wonderful, but not if you are equipped to live. Just existing gives no texture to the fabric of our lives, no joy, no satisfaction. Not for a human being. To exist but not live is like owning a great sports car but never driving it, having a pool but never swimming in it. Time is for more than just holding on to.

Have you ever seen children dipping a little wand into soapy water and waving it quickly through the air to form a large, transparent bubble, which then floats free? I like to envision time as that bubble. Each year, each day, each moment, every one of us receives a new bubble of time. The past is comprised of those bubbles that have come to us and then floated off in the wind at night. The future is comprised of the bubbles we will receive in coming moments, days, years.

Too many of us believe that life is a time only for receiving and holding bubbles. We grasp them in our hands, look at them, protect them so that they don't pop and get all over us, and then we let them go. As the years go by, we consider ourself fortunate just to have held a lot of bubbles. We try to stay well and live long enough to hold many more. Counting and holding them is enough.

Or *is* it enough? Do we grow weary of taking the day's bubbles in one hand each morning, holding them for the day, then handing them off to the other hand each night? Sometimes we don't even remember doing it. We become automatic. Eventually our arms grow tired, our hands feel rather empty, our hearts feel sad and unsatisfied.

Time is a gift, a present to us. But it is a present that is different than most; it requires our presence. Without our presence, it is just an opportunity. Each day's bubble of time is like a sports car that suggests, "Jump in!"

When the bubble of each day is handed to us in the morning—delicate, glimmering, tenuous—we need to do more than hold it and pass it on. We need to enter into it. We need to fill it with our presence—our feelings, our awareness, our heart, our very self. If we don't, we stay outside looking in.

Many people who seem to be enjoying life really are not. They are enjoying, rather, the passing of time. They overlook the bubble of today because they are too busy, too distracted, too angry, or too apathetic. When we get right down to it, there's a lot of motion and energy generated every day, but minimal satisfaction. Late at night or when all is silent, many people realize that their bubble of time passed unfilled that day. They were not in it.

We must not just hold time in our hands. We must jump into it. We can't be too afraid we'll break it or look silly. The skin of each day's bubble is not that thick. It yields to us more than we think. It's very pliable. Being pragmatic, computer-oriented people, we ask ourself: "How do I get into the bubble of life? How can I program myself into it?"

We cannot. We can't program ourself to be there, nor force or buy our way in. We can't even be self-conscious. We get inside by forgetting ourself, being less protected, less defensive, and more open. We have to permit life to happen to us. Rather than force our way in, we must allow life to draw us in. We have to let it take our heart and lead it to others with empathy, involve us in situations that make us laugh or cry, cause us suffering and ecstasy, make us doubt and then believe.

Time wants to be a matchmaker and introduce us to life, hoping something will come of it. Time wants to teach us that happiness won't come floating to us in some future bubble of time; it is in the bubble we're holding now. And unless we get our happiness out of who we are, what we are, where we are, and whom we love, we may never know what happiness is. Above all, time wants to introduce us to the timeless, to the mysterious Eternal One we call God. God is really at the core of life. By finding God we find love and life. By finding love and life, we find God.

Tomorrow you will hold a brand new bubble of time in your hands. Listen closely, and you'll hear it say to you, "Come on in!"

Virtus Stat in Medio

BE HEALTHY, we're strongly advised. Watch your weight, exercise regularly, cut down on saturated fats. Do this, but don't do that. A kind of Health Bible is being written. Professionally inspired authorities urge us to believe it and follow it, but we're becoming unsettled by it. The advice is ever changing, sometimes contradictory. More and more we are asked to tear pages out of our Health Bible and insert new ones.

Various findings and studies in legitimate journals of medicine, science, or nutrition frequently make changes in what is healthy and what is not. Confusing! We are advised that two alcoholic drinks a day can be beneficial to our heart, but then comes the finding that two to five drinks a day increases our chances of some cancers. Eat a low-fat diet, but not too low in fat. Athletes were formerly warned against drinking water during events; now that's passé. Eating fish twice a week is wonderful, but many fish carry bacteria from the polluted waters they live in.

As Health Bible followers, we first feel secure about what we're doing, then insecure. "Am I unwittingly hurting myself and my family, or am I doing good?" We can feel foolish.

Instead of living with the uncertainty that depends on the latest findings, which next week may become passé, wouldn't it be nice if the Health Bible could be condensed? What if there were just several nuggets of healthful truths that have been and always will be true? It is said that there are some absolute moral truths. What if there were some absolute healthful truths? And what if the moral and healthful were even interconnected?

113

One of the few constant truths I would offer to be placed in the Health Bible would be, *Virtus stat in medio.* This ancient adage means, "Virtue—or the right thing—stands in the middle." Stated more briefly, "In everything, moderation." In one word, "Balance."

What is best for us usually stands between too much and too little, between excess and defect. It stands between too much fat intake and too little fat, between excessive exercise or the defect of no exercise. It means seeking a middle ground between working too much (thereby neglecting our health, our family, our God) and working too little (so that we are lazy and fail to contribute responsibly and creatively to the world). It means finding the middle ground between thinking of ourself too exclusively and thinking of the feelings and welfare of others too much. The ancients had it right: Everything old is new again—*virtus stat in medio.*

Perhaps such wisdom has been around so long that we have overlooked it. The concept is nothing new. Our body and soul have been geared to this concept for ages. The scientific name for this is *homeostasis,* "the ability of an organism to maintain an internal equilibrium." If our body doesn't get enough water, it becomes thirsty and encourages us to drink more. On the other hand, if we drink too much water, we feel uncomfortable, and our body regurgitates it or seeks to right the imbalance in some other way. If we have no solid emotional relationship, we feel lonely; if we try to have too many, we don't connect well enough with any of them. If our soul is depleted of meaning, we feel empty and unsatisfied. The healthiest humans are those who try to balance their lives—the material part with the spiritual part, the concern for self with the concern for others, work with play.

We can even become unbalanced by trying to be too "religious" in an inhuman kind of way. To reject our own emotionality or attention to healthy human needs makes us too sterile, too antiseptic, not in touch with God, others, or our own true self. We are in danger of becoming what Gerald Vann called an immaculate misconception. We are correct, pure, and proper, perhaps, but not warm, winning, and in touch.

More health dictums will change next week. Just remember that we are complex beings who seek a balanced life. Virtue stands in the middle and calls us to come from the extremes to join her.

Eyes Wide Shut About Sex

WITH OUR EYES WIDE OPEN, we can see so much, but we are often shut to the truth about what we see. Take human sexuality for example. How many of us see it as one of God's greatest gifts and understand and enjoy it accordingly? Theologian Daniel J. O'Leary writes:

> A fog of suspicion still surrounds this rich and amazing gift of the human expression of love. . . . All my memories of past studies of human sexuality have to do with temptations, anxieties and degrees of moral culpability.

To us sex and sin go together, not sex and God.

The history of sexuality is long and complicated, and it is not getting any clearer. Attempts at considering it in a more spiritual way draw suspicion even from spiritually minded people. They fear such terminology is merely a subterfuge offering an excuse for hedonism or sexual license. The Manichaeism that has plagued the human race for three millennia dies hard.

Every so often new movies come along that bring sexuality to the fore. *Eyes Wide Shut* received a great deal of attention because of its renowned director, the late Stanley Kubrick, and megastars Tom Cruise and Nicole Kidman. It may join the ranks of *Midnight Cowboy, Emmanuelle, A Clockwork Orange, Last Tango in Paris,* and other films on sexual themes considered artistically notable.

Despite all the attention sexuality has been given throughout history, we have not yet been convinced that it is more than skin deep. We see sexual activity as a meeting of

115

two sexual bodies but only minimally as a union of two sexual persons. The human race hungers for the meeting of persons in intimate, loving, and committed relationships. We long to share closeness and warmth in a permanent context of vulnerability and openness. When this truly happens, divinity blesses our humanity and God's ecstatic gift is unwrapped totally.

Our cultural values create many obstacles to intimacy. We extol individualism over relationship, self-sufficiency over self-revelation, getting quickly to bed over long-term communication. Paradoxically the longing for intimacy could well be the drive behind the apparent casualness of sexual activity today. Though permissiveness is seen as abandonment to sexual license, it is often a frantic search for intimacy. Behind the apparent sexiness and explicitness of our culture, there lurks a sense of alienation, loneliness, and an absence of meaning. Our solution? We think that by losing ourselves in the *act* of togetherness, we will find *actual* togetherness. The subsequent disappointment leads to more searching. Moral theologian Kevin T. Kelly says:

> In our current climate a truly human sexual ethic will be, to a large extent, counter-cultural. It will be an ethic which swims against the tide of those forms of sexual mores which are deeply influenced by contemporary individualism. One such form, for instance, is a very individualist recreational interpretation of sexuality which views sexual activity as a kind of competitive sport in which the whole object of the game is to gain maximum satisfaction for the individuals engaged in it. As with all competitive sports, it accepts that there will be losers.

It is not God's plan to have losers in a game called sexuality. Perhaps we can hope that future sexually oriented movies will have a corollary effect. Perhaps they will remind us that what we *don't* appreciate about human sexuality is what will keep us lonely. As her era's sexy woman, Mae West said, "Too much of a good thing is wonderful!" Sometimes too much of a good thing makes us tire of it or lose our fullest enjoyment of it. Have you ever gotten sick from some delicious food and then couldn't eat it again for a long time?

Unfortunately because so many parents fear talking about human sexuality with their children, and so many ultraconservatives just keep repeating, "Thou shalt not," and so many liberals say, "No big deal," the day of our full appreciation of human sexuality is still far off.

Is There a God Named Sports?

I ENJOY SPORTS. Earlier in life I played quite a few. Fast-pitch softball was my favorite, and I was quite good at it, as was also the case with handball and racquetball. Those wonderful days are over. Now I enjoy being a spectator, but I still feel the urge to get out there and sweat, compete, and experience the thrill of a well-played game.

Sports offer many benefits to those who participate. Pope John Paul II was an athlete in his youth. In later reflections on the topic, he remarked on the benefits of sports: they contribute to the integral development of the human person; they promote self-discipline and the awareness of one's strengths and weaknesses; they help to instill loyalty, fair play, generosity, friendship, solidarity, respect, and a spirit of cooperation. Sports can strengthen the unity of the human family beyond differences of race, culture, politics, or religion. Pope John Paul II extols sports as being a training ground for life in that they help us deal with adversity and overcome obstacles. We can also learn virtues from sports: courage, self-control, justice, humility, and how to cope with loss.

For half a year, I traveled fifty miles on a busy expressway to celebrate Sunday Mass in a distant parish. As I drove my route in the warm months of the year, I was amazed by the number of people I saw on playing fields along the way. During the traditional church-going hours of Sunday mornings, almost every diamond or field was occupied by youth practicing or playing soccer, football, or baseball.

Friends with children tell me that their kids frequently bring home sports schedules that include Sunday mornings. Coaches tell

117

kids, "Be there this Sunday morning at 9:30, or you won't play next week." Behold the source of so many problems—unthinking adults. Adult coaches ought to know better and ought to have a larger set of priorities, and adult parents ought to have the courage to say to coaches: "What do you mean be here on Sunday morning? That's church time!"

If sports are to live up to their accolades and be a legitimate training ground for life, then we must not lose sight of the fact that some things are more important than sports. The most powerful way to teach young people that God is a reality and that spirituality is an essential aspect of life is by example. Kids need to see that God and time for God are recognized and revered by significant adults in their life. They need to see that God matters to both parents and coaches. Coaches need not be Sunday school teachers, but they sure ought to be Sunday school advocates.

Adolescence is the least religious time of the whole life spectrum. Good parents already struggle to get their kids to attend church. They don't need to be faced with a choice between two important experiences of life—church and sports. When that happens we know what *naturally* wins, despite what is *supernaturally* needed.

Looking beyond the Sunday morning scheduling conflict, do we see other ways in which sports are replacing God? The first of the Ten Commandments says that there is only one God, and nothing else is to surpass this Being as a priority in our life. Some commentators point out that *worship* is the best term to describe the attitude of spectators toward sports. As sociologist Andrew Greeley says, many public sports spectacles have a powerful religious component. We hear coaches, players, and fans use religious terminology such as *spirit, ultimate commitment, dedication, sacrifice.* We see the prescribed rituals, the fanatical supporters, and the miniskirted vestal virgins at games of all kinds. The adoration bestowed on players seems to convince them that they have semidivine status. Games get turned into dramatic imitations of war between the forces of good and evil. Eisenhower joked that an atheist is a person who watches a Notre Dame–Southern Methodist football game and doesn't care who wins.

Sports can make participants proud, arrogant, and superior, or they can help us conquer our fears, expose our false insufficiencies, and make us humbly appreciative. Sports are a wonderful aspect of life in this world. Let's keep them as a benefit, not a detriment.

Respect for Privacy

WITH THE RISE of the information age, all kinds of ethical questions have arisen about the proper use of information. For example, employers see e-mail as a company-owned tool that is to be used for business purposes only. Employees usually think of it as a telephone that can be used for both business and personal reasons. Do employers have the right to know and read all employee e-mail?

Consider computer databases. Computers make it easy to store and retrieve data about practically anything about anyone. Who owns that data? Can it be used without permission by anyone else? Can it be sold?

Or what about how easily conversations on cordless and cellular phones can be intercepted? Strangers or neighbors may know, from our phone conversations with friends and family, what medical problems we have, what prescriptions we have phoned in to the pharmacy, what we have planned for vacation, or the details of relational problems we are having with our children or spouse. Are we just being nosy when we listen secretly and gather and share such information, or are we doing something immoral?

Personal privacy is under siege. At first glance it may seem harmless, and a small price to pay, for the facility of reaching others swiftly and inexpensively. But on a deeper level, the erosion of privacy threatens our sense of personal identity. Not only do we own physical property like our house, our car, and our clothing, but we also own intellectual property—our thoughts and our decisions. We own our heart property as well—our loves, our fears, and our dreams. If we are stripped of these unique elements, we feel violated, intruded upon, angry, and insecure.

When we speak of our identity, we refer to our sense of who we are, the borders and psychological boundaries that make up our person. We have a basic guardianship of our own boundaries. Each of us must decide when and to whom to reveal ourself, and from whom to reserve ourself. The property of our body, heart, and mind can only be freely given, not invaded or snatched. Imagine the slow erosion of this identity and self-respect if we lived in a culture whose technology enabled "communication burglars" to invade our personal domain. Richard J. Severson makes this point in his book *The Principles of Information Ethics:*

> If "Big Brother" denied us all personal privacy, our self-identities would be destroyed just as Winston Smith's was in Orwell's *Nineteen Eighty-Four.* Privacy is one of the necessary ingredients of self-identity. We are the stories that we live and tell about ourselves. The profiles about us that data collectors "own" are rudimentary stories that compete with our own abilities to say who we are.

The solution to such breaches of personal identity is not simply more laws. We must refine our moral instincts. Law, like ethics, must follow morality. There is no more effective way to police the human heart than by moral persuasion—the personal recognition of right and wrong, the healthy and the unhealthy. Whatever our scientific and technological advances, we must adhere to the dignity, rights, and responsibilities of our nature as created by God, and treat ourself and others accordingly. Whether we call it conscience or moral compass, we have the innate ability to recognize right from wrong and to develop an ethical system that embodies our principles. As Severson says, "The purpose of ethics . . . is to make our morality more effective." Part of our disrespect of privacy today flows from the fact that our moral instincts don't function well in situations that are new or complex. Technological advances have outpaced ethical advances. We tend to think that just because we *can* do something, we *may.*

Hard violence is recognizable—rape, murder, physical and verbal assault. Soft violence is often not as recognizable and perhaps not even understood as violence—invading others' personal boundaries, ruining reputations, revealing or trifling with private inner lives. A high-minded culture strives to rid itself of both forms of violence.

God's
Fingerprints

SERENDIPITY—I LIKE THE SOUND of that word, and I like its meaning. What does it mean? A serendipity is an unexpected happy occurrence. Or, as *Webster's College Dictionary* officially defines it, "an aptitude for making desirable discoveries by accident." Many occurrences in our lives seem to be accidental, but others seem to be much more than that. They seem to have meaning, but the cause and meaning can never be proven.

I bet you recall many moments of serendipity in your life—how you just happened to make the right connection that got you a job, how a sudden twist of events led you to attend the university where you met your spouse, how coincidentally you met someone in the medical profession who later benefited you immensely. Such moments come in all sizes, but they do happen.

Some call the whole thing blind fate. Discussing such arbitrary occurrences might seem childish at first, yet in such a well-respected human science as Jungian psychology, the same concept is expressed by the term *synchronicity.* In the language of spirituality, we can call it *grace.*

Carl Jung's word, *synchronicity,* refers to a significant coincidence. His interest was piqued when he saw some things happening outside us coinciding, apparently by chance, with things happening deep within us. Perhaps we think of someone we haven't seen for years, and suddenly a letter from that person shows up in the mail. Causality is inadequate to explain such a phenomenon, so we usually dismiss the occurrence as chance. Doctor Jung speculates that the two events are not causal but are linked by meaning. More technically speaking, he thinks that disparate events can be connected via the unconscious if they participate in the same spiritual or archetypal meaning. So a meeting with someone who later proves to be vital in our lives might appear to be accidental, but it could have been guided by the unconscious operating through synchronicity.

Some of us may speak of this as grace. We may look back and see that the providence of God has worked subtly in our lives. Though we remained totally free throughout these occurrences, somehow they came to pass; we chose without coercion, and they worked to our benefit. A coincidence seems a minor miracle in which God chooses to remain anonymous.

Psychotherapist Robert A. Johnson likes to think of many of these occurrences as "slender threads" touching our lives. He says, "The possibility of the slender threads operating at all times is so staggering that most of us can't bear it." To be aware of them all, he says, requires the "perspective of saint," and not many of us can bear that perspective. "It is probably true that we live in a universe with more meaning in it than we can comprehend or even tolerate. Life is not meaningless; it is overflowing with meaning, pattern, and connections."

Attesting to his own belief in the reality of serendipity, famed psychiatrist M. Scott Peck MD, writes:

> I've become more and more impressed by the frequency of statistically highly improbable events. In their improbability, I gradually began to see the fingerprints of God. On the basis of such events in my own life and in the lives of patients . . . , I know that grace is real. . . .
>
> We who are properly skeptical and scientific-minded may be inclined to dismiss this force since we can't touch it and have no decent way to measure it. Yet it exists. It is real.

In many ways we are enveloped by the arms of God. Before we are even willing to recognize it, God's hand is there, trying to guide, help, lead, and love. Though at times we realize how alone we are, another reality suggests that we are not. God does not play dice with our life. God has a vast eternal plan that freely, yet masterfully, leads us on. Listen, watch, think, and you'll see God in your own life.

Sheeple

SHEEPLE ARE PEOPLE who act like sheep. How do sheep act? They are not clever or courageous. They are creatures that need help and are easily led. Sheep are not good at recognizing familiar locations, so they occasionally wander off and get lost. They are easy prey for wily predators. When helpless or lost, sheep usually panic; they fall to the ground and bleat loudly to solicit help from the shepherd. Their neediness serves as a counterpoint, allowing us to praise the shepherd who protects them, searches for them when they are lost, and guides them to grazing places. Shepherding was one of the earliest occupations. Frequent accounts in the Jewish and Christian Scriptures depict God dealing with people as a caring and protective shepherd deals with sheep.

Sheep are admirable creatures, however. They act out of their nature. Who can blame sheep for being sheep? We would be shocked to see a bird or a human trying to be like a sheep. God gave us a mind that is supposed to make us quite the opposite of sheep. We are to grow and become insightful, we are to develop a set of priorities so that we don't miss the meaning of life, and we are to recognize truth and have the courage to live by it. Our nature also enables us to develop the highest of all qualities—the ability to love others.

As we mature we are supposed to need shepherds less and less. The task of good parents is to become more and more unnecessary to their children. When we are immature and undeveloped, we have great need for guides—parents, disciplinarians, teachers—*outside* ourself. As we grow and mature, we are expected to be able to direct our own lives by the truth we've learned and the love we carry within our heart. In other words the shepherd is supposed to move *inside* us. Outer shepherds never become altogether unimportant, but they are much less necessary.

Too many of us, however, are turning into sheeple. Many of us seem not to be using our own mind to think. We don't seem to be searching for truth—just expediency. We don't look into problems and try to understand and solve them with intelligence and attention to moral considerations. Instead we graze on sound bites, slogans, and little bits of information lying on the ground that taste good. We swallow what pollsters and spin doctors say, no matter what their method or motive may be, and we, as sheeple, take this as the truth.

When we are sheeple, we have a flock instinct. We turn our mind and our morals over to others. That's why we get lost, don't recognize the right paths, and become easy prey for anyone with a little cunning. Sheeple are dazzled by words, and they forget justice; they are moved too much by emotion, and they overlook logic. Sheeple become incensed when a mother throws her unwanted newborn into a dumpster, but they overlook things like partial-birth abortions—a practice just inches short of infanticide. If we use euphemistic, pleasant-sounding words, sheeple will believe what we say. Sheeple believe advertisers and celebrities about what is important in life, and they acquiesce to anyone who claims to speak for God. Sheeple do all this and more.

The masses of people who make up the human race have been pictured as a huge pyramid. Most of us are depicted at the bottom, and the numbers become fewer as the pyramid ascends and narrows. Psychologists like Abraham Maslow speak of the need for us humans toward the bottom of the pyramid to become self-actualized. This means that we should grow up in awareness and knowledge of ourself and the truth of reality. To do so takes a long time, much thinking, and great honesty.

The journey upward is very difficult, but possible. Great teachers like Jesus Christ told us how to transcend ourself and what will happen when we are transformed from sheeple to people: "You will know the truth, and the truth will make you free" (John 8:32).

Free from what? We will be free from the flock mentality and the inability to recognize our own dignity; free from ignorance, deception, and naiveté; free from our own defenses and illusions in order to become our truest selves. We will be free to see clearly from whom we came and to whom we are going—and to know the way there.

You've Come a Long Way— Woman!

PEOPLE FROM PAST CIVILIZATIONS would have been astounded if they had been there. On Saturday, 11 July 1999, a bright, blue-skied, sunny afternoon, 190,185 people jammed into Pasadena's Rose Bowl stadium, making up the largest crowd ever to gather for a women's sporting event in this country, possibly in the history of the world. Another forty million people watched on television. It was the finals for the Women's World Cup in soccer, played between the United States and China.

The game was more than a highly hyped athletic event, however. It, like many other significant historic events, sneaked up on us, happened, and then left us pondering in its aftermath. It became a milestone on the path away from what was, a stepping stone on the way to what is to come.

Unrolling the scroll of world history, especially the history of the attitudes between the sexes, we see that what is happening today is momentous. Most societies in the past have been patriarchal, and as such have considered women inferior. Aristotle thought it took longer for a woman's soul to develop than a man's. He also believed that the "male is by nature superior, and the female inferior; and the one rules, and the other is ruled." Pythagoras proclaimed, "There is a good principle, which has created order, light and man; and a bad principle, which has created chaos, darkness and woman." Saint Paul writes: "I do not permit a woman to teach or to have authority over a man. She must be quiet. For Adam was formed first, then Eve. Further, Adam was not deceived, but the woman was deceived and transgressed" (1 Timothy 2:12–14). Consider the thoughts of Martin Luther: "Men

125

have broad and large chests, and small narrow hips, and more understanding than women, who have but small and narrow breasts, and broad hips, to the end they should remain at home, sit still, keep house, and bear and bring up children." Those men represent the thought of the times at various points of human history. Such "truths" were instrumental in creating the self-images and attitudes that women and men held about themselves.

History teaches us as well that impressive occurrences in one realm of life have their impact in others. The rights for women to vote, to minister to others in religion, to run for public office, to fly military jets, and to compete in athletics are all interwoven. As they evolve they offer a new image of what it means to be a woman, and as well, what it means to be a man. Standing in the midst of the turmoil and change of today, we must ask: Is a new initiation into womanhood arising? And if so, will a new initiation into manhood arise as well? After centuries of grief and repressed anger, are the dreams of women becoming reality? Are humans rising to a new level of equal relationship in which mature man unites with mature woman? If the sages of the past had been sitting in the Rose Bowl Stadium that sunshiny afternoon, what would they have said about the deeper meaning of such games? Would they change some of their opinions, or would they condemn us?

Over the last few decades, men and women have developed a vision of partnership. In friendship, marriage, and work, partners are called on to recognize differing talents as complementary rather than to see them in opposition, some being superior to others. Seen through the lens of partnership, our differences do not just set us apart. They draw us together. They reinforce our need for each other. The talents and characteristics of each sex are not to be feared or repressed but celebrated.

There is something wholesome about females' participation in sports today. Their physical skills and health are enhanced, they add a dimension of enthusiasm to the game, and they connect with fans. It's about time they were on the field. Seeing women enjoy healthy competition and intense play, observing them in such a physical limelight and learning the benefits sports impart, reminds us of what has been denied them for so long. One wants to call out to them: "It's good you're here! Where have you been for so long?" This is a question, however, best left unasked by men. The answer is not gratifying.

Notes

10   Anita Barrows and Joanna Macy, trans., *Rilke's Book of Hours: Love Poems to God* (New York: Berkley Publishing Group, 1996), p. 88.

12   In John S. Dunne, *The Music of Time: Words and Music and Spiritual Friendship* (Notre Dame, IN: University of Notre Dame Press, 1996), p. 153.

13   "Beauty is serene and . . ." Rollo May, *My Quest for Beauty* (Dallas: Saybrook Publishing Company, 1985), p. 20.

13   "When we are before . . ." Ibid., p. 24.

14   "And I said to all . . ." Henry Chadwick, trans., *Saint Augustine Confessions* (New York: Oxford University Press, 1991), p. 183.

14   "Late have I loved . . ." Saint Augustine, *Confessions,* book 10, part 38.

16   Charles Swindoll, Max Lucado, and Charles Colson, *The Glory of Christmas* (Dallas: Word Publishing, 1996), p. 67.

18   Virginia Sloyan, ed., *A Sourcebook About Christian Death* (Chicago: Liturgy Training Publications, 1990), p. 75.

26   Most Rev. Fulton J. Sheen, *Way to Happiness* (Garden City, NY: Garden City Books, 1954), p. 78.

32   John Shea, *The Legend of the Bells and Other Tales: Stories of the Human Spirit* (Chicago: ACTA Publications, 1996), p. 176.

37–38 Harold Kushner, *Who Needs God* (New York: Summit Books, 1989), p. 70.

38   Ibid., p. 71.

44   "The greatest discovery . . ." In Eileen Campbell, ed., *A Dancing Star: Inspirations to Guide and Heal* (London: Aquarian/Thorsons, an Imprint of HarperCollins*Publishers,* 1991), n.p.

44   "All we are . . ." In Wayne Muller, *How, Then, Shall We Live?* (New York: Bantam Books, Bantam Doubleday Dell Publishing Group, 1996), p. 104.

44   "Where you are . . ." Harry A. Wilmer, *Practical Jung: Nuts and Bolts of Jungian Psychotherapy* (Wilmette, IL: Chiron Publications, 1987), p. 129.

49   "Entering psychotherapy . . ." M. Scott Peck, *The Road Less Traveled: A New Psychology of Love, Traditional Values and Spiritual Growth* (New York: Simon and Schuster, 1978), p. 54.

49   "It is because . . ." Ibid.

50   "He prefers the . . ." Sheldon B. Kopp, *If You Meet the Buddha on the Road, Kill Him!* (Palo Alto, CA: Science and Behavior Books, 1972), p. 2.

50   "The therapist is . . ." Ibid.

52   "Doubts are the . . ." Frederick Buechner, *Wishful Thinking: A Theological ABC* (New York: Harper and Row, Publishers, 1973), p. 20.

52   "The truth may . . ." In Rebecca Davis and Susan Mesner, eds., *The Treasury of Religious and Spiritual Quotations: Words to Live By* (Pleasantville, NY: Reader's Digest Association, 1994), p. 576.

57   "Dear God, . . ." Stuart Hample and Eric Marshall, comps., *Children's Letters to God* (New York: Workman Publishing, 1991), n.p.

57   "So we live . . ." In James Hollis, *Swamplands of the Soul: New Life in Dismal Places* (Toronto: Inner City Books, 1996), p. 42.

58   Ibid., p. 43.

61   In Heinz Kohut, *The Restoration of the Self* (Madison, CT: International Universities Press, 1990), p. 287.

68   *Hymns to an Unknown God* (New York: Bantam Books, Bantam Doubleday Dell Publishing Group, 1994), p. 68.

72   In James Hollis, *The Middle Passage: From Misery to Meaning in Midlife* (Toronto: Inner City Books, 1993), p. 94.

73   In John Bartlett, *Familiar Quotations: A Collection of Passages, Phrases and Proverbs Traced to Their Sources in Ancient and Modern Literature.* Edited by Emily Morison Beck and the editorial staff of Little, Brown and Company. (Boston: Little, Brown and Company, 1980), p. 559.

74   John Carmody, *Living with God . . . in Good Times and Bad* (New York: Crossroad Publishing Company, 1996), p. 72.

79   James Hollis, *Swamplands of the Soul: New Life in Dismal Places,* p. 9.

83   Thomas H. Johnson, ed., *The Complete Poems of Emily Dickinson,* (Boston: Little, Brown and Company, 1960), p. 507.

85   In *The Macmillan Dictionary of Quotations* (New York: Macmillan Publishing Company, 1987), p. 140.

86   Henri Boulad, *All Is Grace: God and the Mystery of Time* (New York: Crossroad Publishing Company, 1991), p. 42.

87   In John Bartlett, *Familiar Quotations: A Collection of Passages, Phrases and Proverbs Traced to Their Sources in Ancient and Modern Literature,* p. 455.

88   In Angela Partington, ed., *The Oxford Dictionary of Quotations, 4th ed.* (New York: Oxford University Press, 1992), p. 578.

92   "Have patience with . . ." Stephen Mitchell, trans., *Letters to a Young Poet* (New York: Vintage Books, Random House, 1986), pp. 34–35.

92   "The goal is . . ." In Daryl Sharp, *Getting to Know You: The Inside Out of Relationship* (Toronto: Inner City Books, 1992), pp. 97–98.

100   Ernest Kurtz and Katherine Ketcham, *The Spirituality of Imperfection: Modern Wisdom from Classic Stories* (New York: Bantam Books, Bantam Doubleday Dell Publishing Group, 1992), p. 19.

103   John Powell, *Fully Human, Fully Alive: A New Life Through a New Vision* (Niles, IL: Argus Communications, 1976), pp. 49–50.

104   "The religious person . . ." Adrian van Kaam, *Religion and Personality* (Englewood, NJ: Prentice-Hall, 1966), p. 55.

104   "The haunting fear . . ." In Angela Partington, ed., *The Oxford Dictionary of Quotations, 4th ed.,* p. 457.

108   Pico Iyer, "The Eloquent Sounds of Silence," *Time,* 25 January 1993, p. 74.

110   "Thinking is . . ." M. Scott Peck, *The Road Less Traveled and Beyond: Spiritual Growth in an Age of Anxiety* (New York: Simon and Schuster, 1997), p. 24.

110   "It was the best . . ." In *The Oxford Dictionary of Quotations, 3rd ed.* (New York: Oxford University Press, 1979), n.p.

115   Daniel J. O'Leary, *Windows of Wonder: A Spirituality of Self-Esteem* (New York: Paulist Press, 1991), p. 156.

116   Kevin T. Kelly, *New Directions in Sexual Ethics: Moral Theology and the Challenge of AIDS* (London: Geoffrey Chapman, 1998), p. 150.

120   "If 'Big Brother' . . ." Richard J. Severson, *The Principles of Information Ethics* (Armonk, NY: M. E. Sharpe, 1997), pp. 73–74.

120   "The purpose of . . ." Ibid., pp. 36–37.

121   *Webster's College Dictionary* (New York: Random House, 1991), p. 1223.

122   "The possibility of . . ." Robert A. Johnson with Jerry M. Ruhl, *Balancing Heaven and Earth: A Memoir* (San Francisco: HarperSanFrancisco, 1998), p. 103.

122   "I've become . . ." M. Scott Peck, *The Road Less Traveled and Beyond,* pp. 258–259.

Acknowledgments *(continued)*

The quotation on page 10 is from *Rilke's Book of Hours: Love Poems to God,* translated by Anita Barrows and Joanna Macy (New York: Berkley Publishing Group, 1996), page 88. Copyright © 1996 by Anita Barrows and Joanna Macy. Permission applied for.

The quotation on page 18 is from *A Sourcebook About Christian Death,* edited by Virginia Sloyan (Chicago: Liturgy Training Publications, 1990), page 75. Copyright © 1990 by the Archdiocese of Chicago. Used by permission.

The quotation on page 83 is from *The Complete Poems of Emily Dickinson,* edited by Thomas H. Johnson (Boston: Little, Brown and Company, 1960), page 507. Copyright © 1960 by Mary L. Hampson. Permission applied for.